Teaching Students to Write Effective Essays

MARILYN PRYLE

NEW YORK • TORONTO • LONDON • AUCKLAND • SYDNEY

MEXICO CITY • NEW DELHI • HONG KONG • BUENOS AIRES

Teaching Resources

For my parents, Ernest and Patricia Bogusch, who taught me to love learning.

ACKNOWLEDGMENTS

I am sincerely grateful to the students of East Middle School in Braintree, Massachusetts, and to the administration of the Braintree School District, especially Michael Connelly, Ann Keenan, and Mary Cunningham, for allowing me to learn the art of teaching writing. I also thank my friends and colleagues in Braintree, especially Andrea Gilarde and Dave Wilson, and Mary Heaton, all of whom gave me feedback and support for this project. Finally, I am grateful for Tim, who never wavers, and Gavin and Tiernan, who live the joy of words each day.

"The Quarrel" by Eleanor Farjeon ©Eleanor Farjeon reprinted by permission of David Higham Associates Ltd from *Silver, Sand and Snow* published by Michael Joseph; "We Real Cool: The Pool Players. Seven at the Golden Shovel" from *The World of Gwendolyn Brooks by Gwendolyn Brooks*. Copyright ©1959 by Gwendolyn Brooks. Reprinted by consent of Brooks Permissions. "My Papa's Waltz" by Theodore Roethke from *The Collected Poems of Theodore Roethke* by permission of Doubleday & Company, Inc. Copyright ©1942 by Hearst Magazines, Inc.; "Woman With Flower" by Naomi Long Madgett from *Star by Star*. Copyright © 1965, 1970.

Cover design by Maria Lilja
Interior design by Melinda Belter
Author photo by Joshua Jury

ISBN-13: 978-0-439-74658-8
ISBN-10: 0-439-74658-2
Copyright © 2007 by Marilyn Pryle
All rights reserved.
Printed in the U.S.A.

3 4 5 6 7 8 9 10   31   13 12

Table of Contents

Introduction

Middle school is a wonderful time to be a writer. Early teens, still so close to the unbiased clarity of childhood, start to see with adult eyes, glimpsing the more complex truths that make up our world. It is a border time in life, a time of wisdom. With guidance and encouragement, students can write from that place of border wisdom, using their Janus-like perspectives, which small children cannot understand and full-blown adults can no longer remember. Only middle school students can write what they have to write.

Not all students will become exceptional writers; this is irrelevant. All students can, however, improve the skills they have. In addition, it is my belief that every student can create at least a few pieces during the year that succeed wildly: genuine, interesting, meaningful, polished efforts. And when this happens, the student has not only produced something but also learned something: often we do not know what we think until it comes out of our fingertips. Seeing students grow, not only in writing proficiency but also in personal awareness, is the joy of the writing teacher. What surprises me every year is that I learn something, too.

For many of us, this experience is often tainted by the pressure of standardized testing. Instead of letting students blossom in their own time with meaningful writing assignments, we feel compelled to drill students, usually at the last minute, with canned essay practice in an effort to produce high scores. Creativity and exploration are shelved in favor of one-line writing prompts. We hate it and so do students. In my early years as an English teacher, I felt as if I was betraying students and myself with my two-week test-essay boot camp. A longtime follower of mentors like Nancie Atwell, Lucy Calkins, and Donald Graves, I sought a way to uphold my values as a writer and a writing teacher while helping students do well on the tests.

In 1999, I obtained my dream job, teaching a full-time eighth-grade writing workshop, in the working-class Boston suburb of Braintree. The class was created in response to the new standardized state tests, the MCAS (Massachusetts Comprehensive Assessment System). The curriculum was open: I could teach writing any way I thought best, as long as students performed well on the long-essay portion of the test. I spent the next few years studying sample essays provided by the Massachusetts Department of Education and talking with other teachers who graded the tests during their summers. I created and adapted writing assignments from a variety of sources. I added and cut assignments, revised them, and experimented with their arrangement. The ten assignments in this book are the result. I now have a program that incorporates state-suggested writing skills with my beliefs about choice, authenticity, and the habits of effective writers.

The main difference between my program and traditional test preparation methods is that I use actual genres that one might come across in a newspaper, book, magazine, or mailbox, rather than packaged essay questions that bore students and do nothing to make them think or write more deeply. Furthermore, students actually enjoy writing these assignments. They are excited, for example, to receive letters and even phone calls in response to their letters for social change (Assignment 5). Another difference is that many of these assignments can help prepare students for other sections of the test. For example, one cannot write a book review (Assignment 6) without becoming familiar with the major elements of fiction; one cannot analyze a poem (Assignment 10) without first studying other poems and their characteristics. This kind of information will be handy during the multiple choice literature portions of the test. Finally, these ten assignments prepare students for high school level writing, research and thinking; practice essay questions from a state's education Web site can't do that.

The ten assignments and accompanying mini-lessons are specifically arranged to build on skills as they are acquired. The first three assignments, the Introductory Letter, Process Essay, and Compare and Contrast Essay, are meant to instill confidence, acquaint students with a workshop setting, and teach some basic writing skills that will be reiterated throughout the year. These first assignments also cover the some of the easier essay genres: describing, explaining, and comparing and contrasting. Once students are familiar with classroom procedures and some of the groundwork of essay writing, we begin the art of persuasion, and spend five assignments on it. No two assignments are alike, however, and this variety keeps students' interest high. Finally, the last two assignments are in-depth analyses, which by nature call for a refined sense of persuasion; by that time, students are quite comfortable with skills such as writing introductions and conclusions, organizing, and using rich language, so they can concentrate on the more complex thought that these two assignments require.

I give these assignments throughout the year, so that students have an opportunity to internalize the skills they learn; we don't just cram for the test. There is no quick path to good writing or to high test scores. Given time, students can experiment with structure, language, and thought, and approach the test with a sense of ownership of voice and confidence in their abilities.

You will notice that my methods are ultra-structured: this is because I have nearly a hundred students split into five classes a day. It is not the ideal writing workshop situation, but for many of us, it's the reality. I use an organized, step-by-step approach that accommodates all the needs of my situation, including keeping track of all of the students, reading all their work, making individual suggestions for revisions, reading the revisions, and generating numerical grades for the whole process, on top of making sure students are prepared for the standardized tests in the spring.

But logistics is not my only reason for maintaining this tight structure. For most students, many of the genres are new. Teaching students step by step, holding their hands in a sense, seems like good teaching. Yes, the ultimate goal is to have students who create their own paths as writers; they need, however, a place to start, a place to later divert *from*. They need to master, or at least be familiar with, what's been done a thousand times so that they can someday take it a step further. A six-paragraph persuasive essay may not be the most exciting way to persuade experienced readers, but it's a way to learn the ropes of persuasion. Should it be hammered into their brains throughout high school? Of course not. But at the middle school level, it's a beginning. The struggling students especially appreciate this method.

Even though I determine the genre of each assignment, students always choose their own topics. With every assignment, they write about what is important to them, what interests them, what they like. They employ choice and authenticity every time, a principle espoused by Calkins and Atwell.

Introduction

This not only keeps students motivated but gives them freedom within the structure, an effective formula for learning.

Since I conduct my class as a workshop, most of my time is spent individually conferring with students. Therefore, I always have the opportunity to tailor the assignments to suit individual needs. I regularly exercise my right as mentor and creator to add or omit elements of each assignment depending on the student. Sometimes I let a creative student take off in the direction that pulls him; sometimes I reel him in. Sometimes I nudge a cautious student to experiment; sometimes I let her remain within the safety of the assignment parameters. I can decide. We can decide together.

I continue to work with the assignments and try new strategies when inspiration hits. Like other arts, teaching is organic and always evolving. But my hope is that the assignments presented in this book can help other teachers in situations similar to mine, who have large numbers of students and little time; who must prepare students for standardized essay tests and the requirements of high school writing; who must provide for fair, uniform grading of all students but want to leave room for creativity and personal judgment.

CHAPTER 1

How to Use This Book

How you will use this book depends on your time constraints, class sizes, school curriculum, and, of course, your own judgment. I developed the program while teaching eighth graders; however, all assignments are easily adaptable to various age and skill levels throughout middle school and high school.

If you are solely a writing workshop teacher, as I am, you can move straight through each assignment over a semester, or you can spread the assignments throughout the year, keeping their order, but mixing in poetry, autobiography, and fiction. If you are an English teacher, I suggest starting in September and working an assignment into your curriculum every few weeks.

In each of the ten assignment chapters in this book (Chapters 4–13), I give a brief introduction to the assignment—describing the assignment itself, the mini-lessons, and any other pertinent information. Each chapter includes the actual assignment/grading sheet, any prewriting forms, and any reading materials involved in the assignment. Some of the reading materials were written by professionals, but most are pieces written by former students. I recommend using your own student work as models as well. On all assignment sheets, I call the model reading "sample essays" so you can use my samples or any others you choose.

There are three mini-lessons per assignment; ideally, at least three days in a workshop setting should be devoted to each assignment. I know this may seem like a lot to ask, but three days is the minimum requirement in order to provide sufficient mini-lesson and writing time. If necessary, parts of the assignments can be given for homework, to optimize the three class days. After the three days, another day or two should be reserved for conferencing once the papers start to come in. In an English class, these conferencing/revising days can be scheduled a few days after the writing days if need be, and can themselves be spread out with a day or two between them. Full-time writing teachers can run a continuous workshop. Obviously, your decision about which mini-lessons to use or omit will be based on your own class's needs. But remember that the key to all learning is practice and repetition. The mini-lessons in the early assignments should be reinforced in every subsequent assignment, and students should be held accountable for those skills. For example, writing a strong introduction on a standardized test essay will be much easier for a student if he has successfully done it nine times instead of just once or twice. Thinking of a more specific word than *good* will be second nature when a student has done it for months over the course of writing ten essays.

However you decide to use the contents of this book, I encourage you to read the entire book before taking action, so you have an idea how the assignments and mini-lessons progress, and which will best suit your students.

THE CLASSROOM

I strongly recommend a workshop setting for these assignments, as this will allow students to work at their own pace and for you to meet with each student individually. Many of the following suggestions about workshop procedure and set-up are ideas adapted from Nancie Atwell's *In the Middle* (Heinemann, 1998), a definitive guide to reading and writing workshops at the middle school level.

Students should have two writing folders, one for works-in-progress, and one "permanent folder" for finished pieces, which can be kept in a filing cabinet or crate in the classroom. The permanent folders are invaluable during parent conferences and grading time. I like to have students staple a "Writing Record" inside their permanent folders so they can record the assignment number, title, genre, and date of each piece as it is filed.

If you are fortunate enough to have computers in your classroom, they will be a tremendous asset. Computers are vital to the revising stages of this program. If you only have a few computers in your room, you can set up a rotating schedule. If you do not have any computers in your room, have students type all assignments at home; set up a schedule of in-school computer use (in the school library, for example) for students who don't have computers at home.

For a full-time workshop, I recommend arranging all the assignments and their corresponding materials in clearly marked folders in an "assignment crate" that is easily accessible for students. That way, students can work at their own paces through the assignments and help themselves to new assignments once old ones are finished. In addition, I keep separate shallow bins for an unending supply of Editing/Revising Check Sheets and Spelling Practice Sheets. Other useful materials for a writing workshop include different-colored highlighters, scissors, tape, pens, hundreds of paper clips, and plenty of loose-leaf paper.

On my desk, I have small wire bin labeled "Papers to Be Graded"; next to it, taped to the desktop, I have an index card labeled "Handing-In Order." This card is so useful that I am tempted to shellac it to my desk. It lists the order I want all the papers arranged in for all assignments. Of course, some students need to consult this card up until the last week of school.

Finally, I like to use the entire room as both a reference and a source of inspiration. I hang signs, mostly homemade, which remind students of grammar points and frequently misused words. Smaller signs display rules like "*A lot* is two words (like *a little*)." A large poster has a list of commonly confused homophones that computerized spell checkers won't pick up. Similarly, there is a list of contractions and their homophones (for example, *who's* = *who is*; *whose* is possessive). I hang signs around the room listing the "banned words" in the class—more on this later. And we've got a store-bought poster that explains all marks of punctuation. Many of these topics are covered in

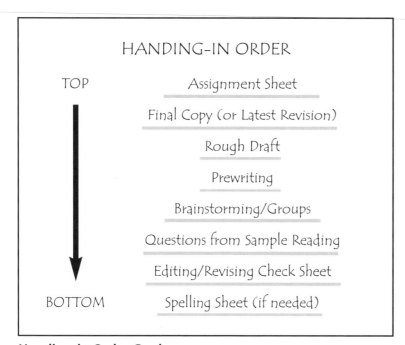

Handing-in Order Card

HANDING-IN ORDER

TOP — Assignment Sheet

Final Copy (or Latest Revision)

Rough Draft

Prewriting

Brainstorming/Groups

Questions from Sample Reading

Editing/Revising Check Sheet

BOTTOM — Spelling Sheet (if needed)

mini-lessons at some point during the year. Additional signs go up after certain mini-lessons. For example, after a mini-lesson in which all my classes generate a list of alternatives to the word *said*, I post the cumulative lexicon as a reference. My hope is that all of this information will sink in over the year—either consciously or subconsciously—and students will have internalized it by the spring.

On the inspirational side, I put up around the room postcard-size photos of famous writers. Below these I list the writer's name, dates, major work(s), and possibly a brief quote. I have accumulated enough pictures so that I can hang one over every computer. Then, if students are daydreaming or trailing off, at least they can learn something while doing so. And since each student is assigned

to a computer, she becomes very familiar with the writers in her vicinity. I feel as if I send them on to high school with at least a few names and works in their heads. Some quotes are meant to inspire: "If there's a book you really want to read but it hasn't been written yet, then you must write it" (Toni Morrison). Some are for cheerleading: "Many times I feel empty, without ideas—and then suddenly the first sentence appears" (Octavio Paz). Still others are to instruct: "The author must keep his mouth shut when his work starts to speak" (Fredrick Nietzsche). For a wealth of wonderful quotations from writers, I suggest Donald M. Murray's *Shoptalk: Learning to Write with Writers* (Heinemann, 1990), as well as the list of quotes that appears in the back of Atwell's *In the Middle*.

CHAPTER 2

Up and Running

The Workshop in Motion

The format of a workshop is simple once it is established. When students finally catch on, the class runs almost by itself. It is wonderful to see students going about their work, focused, moving around the classroom comfortably; visitors are often surprised that middle school students can operate in this type of environment. The key to achieving this is to consistently reinforce all processes and boundaries. In the beginning, I'm on them every step of the way: I explain and re-explain procedures, I take points off any task that is skipped, and I tolerate no disruption or conversation. After a couple of assignments, it all pays off.

When a workshop is in full swing, it looks something like this:

♦ The bell rings, and students are in their seats, notebooks ready; I start the day's mini-lesson.

♦ After the mini-lesson, students begin the assignment or pick up where they left off during the previous class. In an ongoing workshop, students can begin the next assignment once they have completed the one they're working on. In an English class with writing workshop blocks sprinkled throughout the year, some other work should be prepared for students who may finish early.

♦ Students check off completed tasks on the assignment sheets as they work. Each assignment consists of reading some models, answering questions about the models, prewriting, writing a rough draft, typing a final copy and completing an Editing/Revising Check Sheet.

♦ Students work both at their desks and computers, depending on where they are in the assignment.

♦ I circulate around the room, conferencing and doing some mild policing.

♦ When an assignment is finished, the student gathers all her papers and brings them to my desk. There, she puts them in the proper order, paper-clips them, and leaves them in the Papers to Be Graded tray.

♦ If I return to a student a paper that needs further corrections and revisions, he could work on it right away, or save it for later (if he is in the middle of writing another assignment).

♦ If I return a finished paper to a student, she should retrieve her permanent folder from the filing cabinet, replace the paper clip with a staple, record the piece in her Writing Record, and return the file.

♦ Later in the class, I might sit at my desk, reading papers and being available for questions.

♦ Students can approach me with any question whatsoever. They can help themselves to information in any book or poster. They can also help themselves to the Editing/ Revising Check Sheets and Spelling Practice Sheets when needed.

♦ I give students a two-minute warning before the end of class, so they can log off the computers, file any papers, and gather their notebooks and other materials.

The following sections explain aspects of the work-shop in detail.

GRADING

I include the grading rubrics on the bottom of every assignment sheet so that students can see exactly what they are accountable for even before they begin writing. They can also see how the rubrics match the tasks listed on the assignment sheet. The rubrics have evolved through years of trial and error. I have finally settled on five categories—structure, process, description, spelling, grammar—that are flexible enough to tailor to any assignment and broad enough to make students accountable for every step. Even though all of the assignments presented in this book are essays, these categories allow for subtle variations among them. The categories also clarify grades for parents and administrators, while leaving room for my own judgment. Each of the five categories is worth 20 points.

Grading Criteria

STRUCTURE

PROCESS

DESCRIPTION

SPELLING

GRAMMAR

For each assignment, I also list specific skills within each category (see page 13 for an example). By doing so, I can highlight certain requirements for each assignment. And when I grade, I can circle the particular skill that needs work. If a skill is not on the list, I can note it in the margins near its category. Since the Grammar category is so large and most often the source of lost points, I list a few of the most common mistakes and then leave a blank line so that I can fill in any additional skill that requires attention for that student on that assignment.

For most "errors," I subtract 5 points each, with a limit of 20 points per category. After 20 points is lost in any category, I just put a dash on that category's grading line, instead of a "0." Students know exactly where the points are going, and exactly what they have to revise. Through revision, each student can get every point back. And students can revise as many times as they want—

sometimes the same paper gets passed in four or five times. Therefore, each student has the potential to receive a 100 on *every single* assignment. This is enough to motivate most students. For the rest, I have a rule that they must receive a 90 or above on each assignment in order for it to count. Some students want to quit once they achieve 70 points on an assignment, but I see my role not only as instructor but also as coach, pushing students to do their best even when they don't feel like it. I know of other teachers who are using this system who set their lowest acceptable final grade at 80. You may not want to set a minimum grade at all, letting students determine when to stop revising an assignment. Obviously, it depends on you and your students.

Let me here add, and emphasize, that I can make students accountable for as much, or as little, as I wish. For example, if a student has difficulty spelling due to a learning disability, I might only grade the spelling in the student's first paragraph, and give the student specialized practice activities with only those words. Or I may isolate misspelled words throughout the paper that have a similar orthographic pattern and help the student with that one pattern. My grading rubric is not designed to overwhelm students but to push them to do the best they can—and, yes, this is different for each student. The rubric allows for individual skill level. It is my responsibility to learn what those levels are. Below are the five categories explained in detail.

Structure This category accounts for any of the following: organization, length, paragraphs, special formats (as in a letter), and font size. This ensures that students write as much as I want them to—a minimum of one typed page, in 12-point double-spaced Times New Roman, with default margins. Why so specific? Because most middle school students will alter any of these if it means less work. I set a minimum length for the assignments because the more writing there is, the better the chance that the student will hit upon something—or many things—that we can build on towards a finished piece. Certainly, students can write more than a page. If a student is actually writing too much for an assignment, I will tell him to limit his pages to a certain number, or I will help him narrow his topic. This category also accounts for individual paragraph structure and overall organization and order.

Process This category allows me to grade students on completing the steps leading up to the final draft. In the beginning of my tenure, many students wanted to simply write the final draft, to get it done in twenty minutes, without thinking about anything new. I believe the steps, which always include reading and thinking about models (which I check by seeing that written questions are completed), prewriting, and writing a rough draft, are crucial. Often students try to hand in a rough draft and final copy by simply clicking "print" twice. I am able to make them actually revise their rough drafts by making revision part of the grade.

In the beginning of the year, I have students hand-write their rough drafts; as the year progresses, I allow students to type their rough drafts if they wish. Prewriting, however, must always be done by hand. I emphasize using at least some handwriting per assignment for two reasons. First, most of the students will have to handwrite the standardized test essay on test day. I have a colleague who has his students handwrite everything, from prewriting to final draft, for the assignment just before the test, so that students are prepared for the amount of writing involved. But more importantly, I believe that something magical happens in the brain when thoughts travel out one hand and onto paper held by the other hand. There is a connection that doesn't exist with a keyboard and computer screen. So, to strengthen this connection, I have students handwrite the first few rough drafts, and continue to handwrite all prewriting. (This obviously does not include students who have a typing requirement as part of their education plans.)

With the categories of Structure and Process, I use my judgment when it comes to how many points to subtract. For example, not completing the questions for an assignment will cost the student ten points instead of just five. The same is true for prewrites and rough drafts. The skills for any of the categories do not have to add up

to 20; 20 is just the number at which I stop subtracting, so that a student will never get a 60 solely based on, for example, punctuation.

Description This is a broader category that includes skills ranging from using sensory details and strong verbs to having an effective conclusion. The skills in this category may vary from assignment to assignment, based on the genre itself and also what I've taught in the mini-lessons. Again, the bigger the skill, the more points I give it: if a paragraph needs one more example, I might subtract five points, but if someone hands in an essay absolutely devoid of an introduction, I'd take ten points off. Individual student differences play a role, too: if a lower-level student tries some new verbs, even though those verbs aren't the best choices, I'd congratulate her. A more advanced student who uses those same verbs without much thought or effort might lose five points and be sent back to revise them.

Spelling With an exception for students with learning disabilities that affect their ability to spell, my motto is this: I don't care how it happens, but don't let your paper make it to my desk with spelling mistakes on it. Today, spelling is not a matter of talent; it is a matter of motivation. It does not take any effort at all to run a spell-check on the computer, and it takes little effort even to use a dictionary. As of the time of this printing, students in Massachusetts are allowed to use dictionaries during the long essay portion of the MCAS. If I can get students to consult the dictionary repeatedly during the year, they will feel comfortable using one during the test.

In addition to subtracting five points per misspelled word, I have students write out the word five times on a piece of paper to be handed in with their revisions. Students use the Spelling Practice Sheet that is included in Appendix A. This is not so much a punishment as it is a practice: I tell students that at times, misspelling a certain word is a bad habit that they have to break, like nail biting. Of course, writing out a word five times is also an extra motivation to overcome laziness: in the first years, before I had students complete Spelling Practice

		Preliminary Grade	Revised Grade
STRUCTURE (organization, paragraphs, length, font)	20 pts.	_____	_____
PROCESS (brainstorm, rough draft, E/R Check Sheet)	20 pts.	_____	_____
DESCRIPTION (details, intro, conclusion, banned words)	20 pts.	_____	_____
SPELLING	20 pts.	_____	_____
GRAMMAR (punctuation, capitals, sentences, _____)	20 pts.	_____	_____
	TOTAL		_____

Sample Grading Rubric

Sheets, students would ignore spelling while they wrote and let me circle their spelling mistakes, since they always had a chance to revise and get the points back. After I instituted the Spelling Practice Sheet and students had to actually write the words an extra five times each, they miraculously became better spellers. This also saved me precious grading time.

Grammar This is another broad category, which can include as much or as little as I choose. Some skills are always required, like punctuation at the end of sentences. Some skills are learned in mini-lessons and are a focus for that particular assignment. While higher-level students are at times accountable for more, I might keep lower-level students focused on the basics. As with the first three categories, I list any special grammatical skills for each essay, such as quotation marks for the cited quotation in the Personal Essay or underlining book titles in the Book Review.

The grading rubric, then, appears at the bottom of every assignment sheet and generally looks like the one in the sample (see above).

Notice that there are two columns for grades—one for the first draft and one for the revision. I never total the first grade, what I call the "rough" or preliminary grade, since having a 50 or 60 in writing on one's paper would be discouraging. I emphasize to students that these rough numbers are only a starting point. Some students, adding up the numbers in their heads, panic at first. But after the first few assignments, when students

see 90s, 95s, and 100s coming back on their revised papers, they begin to relax and get into a rhythm. The rough grades keep them motivated, however, for each assignment. For students who revise three or more times, I simply continue to cross out that category's old grade and write the new one to the right of it.

As you can see, there is plenty of room for a teacher's personal judgment in this system. At the same time, I have all the numbers I need to show a student, his parents, or my principal.

THE WORKLOAD

I'll be honest about the grading: it takes time. This is the nature of a workshop. I say "grading" but I mean *reading*. As described above, the numbers are never permanent. Usually, I merely circle grammar or spelling mistakes without any further notation. I want students to figure out—on their own, by using a reference book, or by asking me—what the problem is. Structural suggestions need to be written out. If the issue is too large to describe on paper, I'll write a "See me" accompanied by a note to myself so I'll remember what to discuss in a future conference. I try to write as much positive feedback as possible, highlighting specific accomplishments, such as "Strong intro," "Great transition word," "Excellent semicolon!" or "Powerful example." And at the end of each paper, I write a quick sentence that is always encouraging.

A paper that has been corrected once already does not take long to reread, since the latest revision is always atop the earlier corrected copies and all I have to do is flip between them. Reading revisions is actually quite enjoyable: I am already familiar with the paper and do not have to wade through it, and I get a true sense of the student's understanding and progress. It is rewarding. And most papers that come in for a third or fourth time require only a glance, since by then the student is fixing small spelling or grammatical errors. A practical note: With each new draft that a student hands in, I always use a pen of a new color. This makes it easy to keep the drafts in order.

DESK TIME AND CONFERENCING

I'm only at my desk for a portion of the period, but it is a crucial portion. The length of time varies with the class: with a smaller class I may be at the desk more than with a larger class, although sometimes I take advantage of the smaller class size to have longer individual conferences. I think desk time is important for two reasons. First, a student who has a question can approach me without disturbing another student's conference. Second, I get a few minutes to grade papers that have been handed in. Since the desk time comes after I have visited all or most of the students, I never feel guilty about this. Grading is integral to the running of the workshop: if I don't read the papers, the class comes to a halt. And with nearly one hundred students, I cannot read all papers outside of school hours. Some days I have more time to grade; some days I have less or none at all. The conferences always come first, but grading has a place during class.

I usually conference by first talking with students as I return their papers. Not all students have papers coming back to them each day, so this method covers only a portion of the class; I visit the other students after I have returned that day's papers. I go over the paper with the student to make sure he understands my corrections and suggestions; this can entail any number of topics from organization to grammar to thinking of a

title to scrapping the whole second half of an essay and starting again. Of course, I also try to encourage the student as much as possible. I have found that my honest and specific encouragement, both verbal and in writing, has a tremendous impact on most students' quality of writing and productivity. Undoubtedly, this is a basic rule for all teaching, but at the busy times I have to remind myself.

If the paper is finished, I spend a minute praising the finished work and the student's cumulative efforts. Then, I take a quick look at what she is working on at the moment and ask if she has any questions. Since the answer is usually "No," I ask her to tell me about what she is writing or to read me a paragraph. I make a suggestion or two if I have them, but if I don't, I let the student work in peace. I continue around the room in this way until I have seen all or most of the students. If it is the first day of an assignment and all the students are just getting started, I give them time to at least get into a rough draft before I interrupt them.

In general, I like to check up on students but not bog them down with my direction during the creative process. If I have a paper to return to them, I spend a longer time conferring than if I do not. But since they've already "lost" writing time during the mini-lesson, I don't want to take up more of it with my talking. If a student is engrossed in writing, hunched over his desk or staring intently at a computer, I just let him write! Sometimes, even if I have a paper to return to a student but I can see that she is absorbed in her writing, I hold off on returning the paper until the next day. Conversely, if I see that a student is stuck or daydreaming, I attend to him first to help him refocus or switch gears if I have a paper to return.

The topics of the conference vary; they are dictated by students' writing. Sometimes, I find a student struggling with the mini-lesson and I take a couple minutes to go over it again with her. Or a student may have a grammatical bad habit that we work for months to shake. We may work on structure, organization, generating details, spelling mnemonics—anything that would improve the student's writing. I like to give as many examples as I can and sometimes refer to other texts for help. Sometimes I ask another student in the room (quietly, to avoid disturbing others) if I can use his paper as an illustration. This has the dual benefit of encouraging the one student while piquing the curiosity of the student I'm trying to help. Likewise, I have a trove of writing, from both professionals and former students, to use as examples for any student I think will benefit from them.

If a student has to make a number of revisions, I keep her focused on the basics instead of bombarding her with dozens of suggestions; as a result, I have to let some mistakes slide for a while. For example, a student and I may spend days getting the organization of a piece together, and I might then overlook the fact that the piece changes tenses four times in the final paragraph. If I think we have the time to go over the tenses, I will; if the student is falling behind or is starting to tire of the piece because we are beating it to death, I let the tenses go, resolving to get to them in another piece. In short, I let my judgment and expertise guide me.

Sometimes conferences involve cutting apart paragraphs with scissors in order to teach a student about structure, or having a student highlight the entire work in three different-colored markers to explain organization. Sometimes I take out a grammar book so the student can examine a few examples of correct semicolon usage. Sometimes I draw charts or diagrams or stick figures. There is no exact formula for how to run a conference except this: help the student. Make him feel that he's doing a good job and that you recognize his efforts. Get him back on track if he's slacking. Show him you're genuinely interested in his stories, ideas, and feelings, and you want to help him communicate them.

NOTEBOOKS

Students take notes on what is discussed during mini-lessons. They will need to revisit much of this information during the year, since the assignments build on what has been learned. But I also hope that students will look at these notes during high school and even college when needed.

For this reason, I like to keep the mini-lesson notes in a separate notebook. We set up a Table of Contents before beginning any assignment, a wonderful idea suggested by Atwell, which was long before ingrained in me by the nuns back in grade school. Throughout the year, students keep track of the mini-lesson topics and page numbers. The first entry will be "What Is an Essay?" explained in the next chapter. (Students do not use the notebooks for prewriting or rough drafts, all of which must be handed in.) I try to find space in the classroom to keep this set of notebooks so they are not lost or forgotten in lockers. At the end of the year, I implore students to save the notebooks for a year at least, as a test, just to see if they need to look something up. I am confident that within that year, students will quickly realize what a valuable asset the notebooks are and be self-motivated to preserve them. Possibly, students will never again have such a concise survival guide to essay writing.

MINI-LESSONS

Many of the mini-lessons in this book are not "mini" at all. Depending on your schedule, you may want to break some up over two or even three class periods. What is imperative is that the mini-lesson not run so long that students don't have time to write that day. I have had to curb my impulse to over-explain and to barrage students with examples. I present the basics, make sure they take notes, and follow up in individual conferences. I have found that I can keep most mini-lessons under 15 minutes, and many under 10, leaving students with at least 30 more minutes to think and write.

I am especially tempted to go long during grammar mini-lessons. Some students find grammar confusing; I try to stop myself from standing at the board and offering loads of fabricated examples. Instead, I present the mini-lesson concepts in the clearest, most concise way possible, and during the conferences focus on the actual grammar they use in their drafts. I reassure myself that learning grammar conventions is a process for most of us; for now, my goal should be to lay the groundwork with exposure and some practice. If students don't get it right away, that's okay—someday it will all click.

I help students with as many grammar problems in their drafts as possible, without regard to my mini-lesson schedule. For example, if a student's Assignment 1 is riddled with run-ons, I will explain the rule and help him correct it during that first week of writing, even though the official mini-lesson on commas and fragments won't occur until Assignment 7. I try to work with each student where she is; the grammar mini-lessons serve only to remind students of the most common mistakes and to reinforce what we do in individual conferences.

EDITING/REVISING CHECK SHEETS

Every three assignments, I introduce a new Editing/Revising Check Sheet (all of which can be found in Appendix A). I do this for three reasons. First, each new check sheet reflects the more complex topics that are presented throughout the assignments; they evolve as students evolve. Second, I want students to eventually self-check their work with minimal prompting from me, so each check sheet requires students to gradually become more self-reliant. I won't be there during the standardized tests to remind them what they should be checking for; nor will I be there in ninth grade when they have to write five-page story analyses on their own. Finally, students get bored with only one check sheet, and soon memorize it. After a few weeks, many students whip through the check sheet, blindly writing the "answers" they think I'm looking for. By changing the check sheets, I make actual reading a necessity.

The first Editing/Revising Check Sheet is extremely simple; while learning the structure of the workshop, students have enough to think about in the beginning of the year. The check sheet touches upon the organizational and grammatical basics, as well as the "banned words" rule presented during the first assignment.

The second E/R Check Sheet asks students to look more closely at their work, and it incorporates some of the earlier mini-lessons. At the bottom of this check sheet is a blank line for each student to note a personal area of improvement. Students must begin to evaluate their own skills and habits.

The third E/R Check Sheet requires students to use the writing lingo they've learned in the first half of the assignments. It also focuses on pinpointing those mistakes that the student continues to make. There are two blank lines at the bottom for self-evaluation.

The final E/R Check Sheet, used during the last assignment, is almost totally autonomous, listing only three main categories, with blank lines for the student to fill in particular skills. At the bottom, the student must identify the problem areas he has been working on all year. Thus, students go into the state tests, and into high school, knowing what conventions exist and knowing their own strengths and weaknesses.

A Note About Peer Editing

I rarely allow peer editing. I've tried to train students to be effective peer editors, with some success, but in the end I've decided that it's not worth the time that it requires. First, it takes a lot of work to get students past saying that their peer's piece of writing is anything other than "good." Often, middle school students are afraid to critique their peers. Second, all students want to peer edit with their friends, and thus the peer editing conference becomes fertile ground for chatter. I then have to enforce whispering and subsequently hover around students to make sure they are discussing their work. It all takes up too much time and energy that could be spent more constructively. However, that said, I do recognize the value of effective peer editing and hence save it for the final assignments, when students are well versed in both editing and revising techniques as well as the rules of the class. I let students request a peer conference, and I allow it on a case-by-case basis; if I know that nothing but talk will come of the meeting, I veto the request or suggest other students as partners for the two who have approached me.

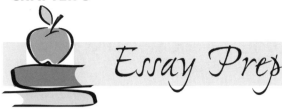

CHAPTER 3

Essay Prep

What Is an Essay?

Before we begin any assignments, I like to take some time to explore the terms *genre* and *essay*. I write "genre" on the board, and before I can ask anything someone usually tries to pronounce it: "Jen-ry? What's that?" It's from French, I explain, and pronounce the word for them. Some of the students realize they have heard it before; one might even remember its meaning. I expound and use music as an example, offering categories like classical, punk, and swing. Soon hands shoot up with the musical genres they know: pop, alternative, rap, hip-hop, hard rock, ska (I had to have this one explained to me), and in short order, I know they've got the concept.

I then ask what writing genres they know. Usually any given class can come up with a list that includes poetry and fiction (they may say "short story" and "novel"). I help them organize terms like autobiography, biography and essays under the umbrella of nonfiction. Someone may even volunteer "script" or "play," since we have *The Diary of Anne Frank* in our eighth-grade curriculum. Someone may even add "newspaper article" and "letter." I list all of these, and circle "essay." This, I explain, is what we will focus on.

One of the most effective ways of defining something is to explore what it's not. I outline a giant chart on the board, with "Essays," "Fiction," "Poems," and "Plays" at the top. Students duplicate the chart in their notebooks and record the topic in their Tables of Contents. I ask them to think of characteristics for each genre that are specific to that genre (this eliminates answers like "uses words"). Students take a few minutes to list what they can; we then discuss their thoughts and develop a master list on the board, which may resemble something like the one below.

I elicit some of these ideas by using student answers from another category. For example, if someone claims that plays don't have much description, I ask if any other genres might typically use a lot of description. For the most part, I let certain generalities slide—like the idea that poems are always short or rhyming—for the sake of time and the overall comparison. Or, I modify the idea by adding words like "can" or "sometimes," as in "can be short" or "sometimes rhymes."

ESSAYS	FICTION	POEMS	PLAYS
explain something	made-up characters	rhyming	dialogue without quotes
about real people	plot	sometimes short	stage directions
author's opinion	theme	short lines	meant to be acted
true	not true	sometimes like a puzzle	not much description
describe something	a lot of description	similes	instructions for actors
short (1–2 pgs.)	short or long	can be about anything	split into acts
intro and conclusion	chapter	stanzas	

By now students can see how essays differ from other genres. "But look at the Essays column," I suggest to the class. "It seems that there can be different types of essays—genres within a genre." I help students convert the ideas on the chart into actual essay genres.

There are even more types of essays than these, I explain, and we will be learning about them throughout the year. I ask, "Looking at this preliminary list, however, what are some characteristics that ALL essays share? Look at our original chart for help." Hopefully one person in the class will realize that all essays are nonfiction.

Essay Genres

EXPLANATORY

BIOGRAPHY/ AUTOBIOGRAPHY

PERSUASIVE

DESCRIPTIVE

I add that essays are written from the author's point of view. This is easy to see with persuasive essays, but it is true with other essays as well: the author's voice comes clearly through. A definition of the essay can be gathered:

> **Essay:** A usually short piece of nonfiction written from the author's perspective.

I always like to add that the word *essay* can be used as a verb, meaning "to try." (I emphasize the shift in pronunciation.) I explain that the root of *essay* is "to weigh," meaning to weigh something in one's mind, to test it out, to examine it from different angles. Imagine holding an idea in your mind the way you would hold an apple in your hand, I tell them, turning it, feeling its weight, looking at its color, deciding if it's good enough to eat.

TOPICS FOR WRITING

I strongly recommend using some class time before beginning any assignments to create a list of Topics for Writing. Atwell calls these "Writing Territories." A list of ideas seems nonthreatening to students because it is only a list. There is no pressure of "having to write something," and so ideas come easily. Later in the year, when students must face the blank page, this list is a welcome oasis.

Like Atwell, I share my own list of writing topics with students, and talk them through it. However, I have additionally found that a systematic line of questioning works best for helping students generate a long and interesting list of possible writing topics. (See questions on the facing page.)

I explain what the list is about and assure them that no one will be looking in their notebook to read their lists, not even me. (Come grading time, I glance at the lists to make sure they exist, but that's all.) I then tell them to write down anything that might be an interesting topic to write about. "Think about your own lives," I suggest. Most stall out after a minute or two; some don't know what to write at all. Then I begin asking the questions, slowly, giving them time to write. If they ask how long the answers should be, I tell them they can write whatever they want: a word, a phrase, a sentence or two—as long as they know what it means.

I find that leading them through these questions becomes almost a guided meditation. Since it is the beginning of the year, and this is students' first time putting pen to paper, they all give it a strong effort.

The list itself is invaluable. With every assignment, there is at least one student who says, "I don't know what to write about." And for every one who tells me that, there are five who have already consulted their Topics for Writing, knowing that will be my suggestion to them.

Questions to Help Generate Topics for Writing

1. Who are some important people in your life? Name them specifically. Family? Friends? How about pets? Who are some interesting people in your life? They might be people you are close to, or people who are interesting acquaintances, like the guy across the street who sings a song called "Mr. Pancake" to the tune of "Mr. Sandman" to call his dog home. What makes these people interesting?

2. What are some of your favorite places? Name them. Add a few details if they come to mind. What are some interesting places you've seen, even if you didn't like them? What are some places you hate?

3. What are some of your favorite belongings, things that mean a lot to you? Some jewelry? A necklace, watch, bracelet, or ring? Something in your room? A piece of clothing?

4. What are some of your favorite movies? What are some movies you didn't like? Do you have a favorite play?

5. What are some of your favorite books? Favorite short stories? [It may help to name some from the previous years' curriculums.] Favorite poems?

6. Who is your favorite band or singer? Which ones do you dislike?

7. What in the school would you change, if you could? In the town? What do you wish your town had?

8. What in our country would you change? Any laws or policies? Should any laws be added?

9. What makes you angry or annoyed?

10. What are your hobbies? What are things you know how to do well?

11. At home, what do you know a lot about?

12. In school, what are your favorite subjects? What subjects are easiest for you?

13. Note a time in your life that was sad, scary, or difficult.

14. Note a time in your life that was funny, joyful, or peaceful.

CHAPTER 4

Assignment 1
Introductory Letter

I know: this is one of the oldest assignments known to teachers. And that is precisely why I use it as the first one. Students feel comfortable: they have plenty to write about, and they don't have to share any deep feelings. Plus, I get to learn a bit about them and they get to learn about me. Most students, by eighth grade, have written letters in previous classes, so their confidence level is high. We start with what they know.

Some students may ask if this assignment is actually an essay. Technically, I tell them, it's a letter, but the bulk of the letter is, in fact, a descriptive essay, since they will be describing themselves in an organized way. Not all letters need be descriptive essays or essays at all. This one, however, is.

An easier assignment in the beginning allows for three intense mini-lessons, explained in detail below. The first lesson is on the most effective form of prewriting I know: brainstorming and grouping. Mastering this technique is essential for success on standardized test essays, so I teach it first and have students practice it throughout the year.

Students begin with clear desks and their notebooks to the side; I hand out the assignment sheet (page 21) and some loose-leaf paper. I also hand out a model: a letter of introduction from me to them, and then begin the lesson for Day 1 of this three-day cycle. (Although this book is meant to be a readily reproducible resource, you should write your own letter. I've included mine on page 23, just as an example.)

> ## Suggested Mini-Lessons
>
> ❑ 1 BRAINSTORMING AND GROUPING
>   *(a half-class lesson)*
>
> ❑ 2 BANNED WORDS
>
> ❑ 3 EDITING/REVISING CHECK SHEET
>
> **Materials:** *Copies of page 21 for students.*

Mini-Lesson 1
Brainstorming and Grouping

This is one of the longest "mini-lessons" of the year, and I try to make sure students have enough class time to begin their own brainstorming. I read my letter aloud to them, pointing out where the addresses, date, salutation, and closing go. This is a review for most. I ask how many paragraphs there are. Then I put my "Brainstorming" example (page 21) on an overhead and explain what *brainstorming* means. I ask students to look at my list and determine which ideas go together. As they offer answers, I write them on the overhead in clusters, circling each group. I cross out the idea from the original list when it becomes part of a group. When the groups are assembled, we number them in an order that feels right, and I explain that each group will become a paragraph. We then compare our groups to the finished letter, noting if I added or subtracted anything as I arrived at my final copy. I emphasize that not everything in a brainstorming list must be used; it is important for a writer to brainstorm freely and without censoring himself, knowing he will decide what ideas are superfluous later.

What makes this lesson long is that I usually model an additional brainstorming and grouping session from scratch on the board, using only student ideas. Students add "Brainstorming and Grouping" to their notebooks and copy what we write on the board. We pick a topic, brainstorm it, and group it. This second model can be skipped if students are already proficient in brain-storming.

Students then get started on their own letter, following the steps on the assignment sheet. Since the first step has been done, I tell them to check it off.

BRAINSTORMING

swimming	University of Scranton
biking	camping
Nova Scotia	Philadelphia
moose	three brothers
fishing	love reading
music	woods / parents' house
eagle	red dirt beaches
vacation	Canada's hills / ocean
love writing	mountains in Scranton
plays	love VT and NH
writing class	

Mini-Lesson 2
Banned Words

To begin, I write the following words on the board:

good	awesome	thing(s)
bad	cool	item(s)
great	nice	kind of
sort of	boring	stuff

Then I announce that these words are banned for the entire year. It may sound stifling to ban words on the second day of writing, but I want students to get these words out of their systems right from the start. There are signs around the room listing these words with a big red circle and slash, so students know this is coming. They record these words in their notebooks. I explain to students that we use these words so often that they don't mean much, or rather, they mean too much. As writers, we must communicate our ideas as precisely as we can,

so students must get in the habit of searching for the most accurate words. I give them an example: "The movie was great." For one person, this could mean it had a happy ending; for another, it could mean the opposite. In addition, a major concern of standardized test graders is the use of "rich" language. If students are able to train themselves to replace the words above with stronger words, they will be better prepared for the test.

I assure students that they can go back to using these words after the year is over if they choose. Until June, however, these words are prohibited! Throughout the year, students will correct me if I use any of these words in my speech. These are wonderful teaching moments, as students watch me search for a better word out loud.

I don't bombard them with lots of examples of the banned words in practice, since ample opportunities will arise in their own writing as the year progresses, and it is more effective to work on each student's individual uses. Plus, I want to keep the mini-lesson short so that students can get back to their letters.

Mini-Lesson 3
Editing/Revising
Check Sheet

Some students will be ready for the E/R Check Sheet by the third day. They don't need to take notes on the E/R Check Sheet, but I always have them keep their notebooks at hand, in case they need to consult notes on other matters. I show them where in the classroom the check sheets are kept, and hand one out to each student. (For all subsequent assignments, they will get their own.) I review the E/R Check Sheet with them and encourage them to put as much thought into it as possible, since it will mean less correcting and revising later. I don't tell them that there are different versions of the Editing/Revising Check Sheet in store for them (see pages 89–92). Since this is most students' first experience with an editing check sheet, I don't want to overwhelm them.

Assignment 1

Introductory Letter

☐ Read the letter I have written to you. You are going to write a letter back to me. Follow these steps:

☐ On paper, brainstorm any ideas about yourself that you want me to know. Be specific.

☐ Organize the information into groups. You should be putting together ideas for three to four paragraphs.

☐ Number the groups in the order that seems best.

☐ Write a first draft. Be sure to use a letter format (see my example) which includes the **recipient's address**, the **sender's address,** and a **date. Don't forget to double space!**

☐ Read it and revise it—look for places where you can add some description (sights, sounds, smells, textures, and so on.)

☐ Type up the draft at your assigned computer. Remember that you must use 12-point Times New Roman and the default margins. Double spaced, the paragraphs should add up to at least **one typed page**. Print out your letter.

☐ Complete an E/R Check Sheet. Revise your letter again and print.

☐ Submit a final draft (in the bin on my desk) with your brainstorming, rough drafts, E/R Check Sheet and this grading sheet.

		Preliminary Grade	Revised Grade
STRUCTURE (letter format, paragraphs, length, font)	20 pts.	_____	_____
PROCESS (brainstorm/groups, rough draft, E/R Check Sheet)	20 pts.	_____	_____
DESCRIPTION (details, examples, no banned words)	20 pts.	_____	_____
SPELLING	20 pts.	_____	_____
GRAMMAR (punctuation, capitals, sentences, _____)	20 pts.	_____	_____
	TOTAL		_____

2 Rosemere Court
Roslindale, MA 02131

September 12, 2002

Writing Students
East Middle School
305 River Street
Braintree, MA 02184

Dear Students,

After waiting all summer, I finally get to meet you. As you know, my name is Ms. Pryle, and I will be teaching your writing workshop.

I grew up near Philadelphia, Pennsylvania. Like Boston, Philadelphia is a beautiful city with a mixture of modern and historic buildings. My family's house stands about 40 minutes outside the city, near thick woods and a small pond where we enjoyed ice skating and fishing. My three brothers and I loved it! I went to college at the University of Scranton, which is in a part of Pennsylvania that has miles of rolling mountains.

I like being outdoors, particularly in the mountains. I love biking and camping, especially in Vermont and New Hampshire when I get the chance. When I was in school, I loved swimming and swam on a team for many years. In addition to sports, I also like to listen to music and watch plays. And of course I love reading and writing!

Last summer, I went on a wonderful vacation to Nova Scotia and New Brunswick. I drove through Canada's beautiful green hills on the edge of the ocean. In addition, I saw some red dirt beaches, and spotted some moose and a bald eagle. The eagle was perched on the top of a pine tree, just looking around, its yellow beak curved like a fishhook. I enjoyed Canada so much that I didn't want to leave.

You are fortunate to have a class especially for writing. Most students in our country don't have a special writing class. Writing is a wonderful way to learn more about yourself and the world. I look forward to working with you this year.

Sincerely,

Ms. Pryle

CHAPTER 5

Assignment 2
Process Essay

Like the Introductory Letter, this assignment draws from students' lives and remains well within their comfort level. It is a "how-to" essay; each student will take the reader through a series of steps in a process that the student knows well. Of course, even at this early juncture some students will claim that they "don't know what to write about." I direct them to their Topics for Writing, and emphasize that this assignment need not be about a unique hobby or talent; students in the past have written essays titled "How to Build a Snow Fort" and "How to Make Oatmeal Squares." Usually the blocked students are just a bit nervous about actually choosing a topic; they don't feel they have any skill in their lives that is "good" enough. I stress to all of them that interesting writing is not so much in the topic itself as in the telling of it. This becomes one of my main mantras for the year.

This assignment is placed early in the year not only because it's within students' comfort level but also because it lends itself to mini-lessons about details, introductions, and conclusions. These three topics are standardized-test staples, and can now be practiced throughout the remaining assignments. In addition, students will naturally use simple transition words such as *first*, *next*, *then*, and *finally*. This sets the class up for the third assignment, when more advanced transition words are introduced.

Suggested Mini-Lessons

☐ 1 SENSORY DETAILS

☐ 2 WAYS TO END AN ESSAY

☐ 3 WAYS TO START AN ESSAY

Materials: *Copies of pages 27 and 28 for students.*

Mini-Lesson 1
Sensory Details

I explain to the class a simple truth: effective writers use sensory details. I ask students to tell me the five senses, and I list them on the board. Then I put up a sentence which conveniently includes a banned word:

> The beach was nice.

Together, in their notebooks and on the board, we list words and phrases under each of the five sense categories. They see the difference. I give them another sentence:

> The park was awesome.

I give them a few minutes to list some details and write a showing paragraph for this telling sentence. After about three minutes we stop, in the interest of time, and read one or two of them aloud. Students then begin the assignment sheet.

Mini-Lesson 2
Ways to End an Essay

Students have had a day to prewrite and begin a rough draft, so most have mapped out their essays. In this mini-lesson, we focus on conclusions. Most students already know what a conclusion is, but they are not exactly sure how to write one. When I ask them what should go into a conclusion, most are stumped. Finally, a student will raise her hand and say, "You repeat the main points from before." That's part of it, I respond, but somehow a conclusion should take the essay's ideas one step further. That "somehow" will be different for every essay. As writers, we must look at the entire piece of writing and decide what ending would be best. Sometimes, for example, we don't need to summarize or restate the main ideas; maybe it would be better to end with an anecdote. The writer must evaluate and choose.

I tell students plainly that conclusions take thought and effort. Don't panic if one doesn't come right away. I give them a list of possible options, and I add their input as it is offered. The list ends up looking a bit like this:

Ways to End an Essay

1. Summarize the main points in *different words*. (I review what "summarize" means, and stress that this option should be combined with another of those listed below.)

2. Give an opinion.

3. Give a brief anecdote that illustrates the main points of the essay, or create a scenario that does the same.

4. Personalize the topic by explaining what it has taught you about life, or how your life has changed / is better because of it.

5. Give a statement of general truth, such as "One must follow his or her conscience" or "People will find time for what is important to them."

6. Give a solution to the problem.

7. Pick up where you left off in the introduction, thereby creating a frame for the entire piece. (I don't try to illustrate this one until the next class, when we will talk about introductions.)

It is difficult to fully explain these techniques without an actual essay to relate to, so I have students copy the list in their notebooks for referral throughout the

year. Different assignments will require different conclusions. I suggest to students that for their Process Essays, they may want to try number 4. During the next assignment, the Compare and Contrast Essay, I will recommend number 3. Number 6 is a classic technique for concluding the Persuasive Essay, and number 5 may be appropriate for the Personal Essay. But these recommendations are not orders; I encourage students to try anything that seems interesting to them, and to try it with confidence. Somehow, though, they must do something new at the end of their writing. They cannot simply repeat what they have already said. On the MCAS, this is one of the crucial differences between advanced and average essays.

The student who wrote about building snow forts concluded by explaining that this activity had taught him patience and focus; a well-made fort that withstands attack cannot simply be thrown together. The author of "How to Make Oatmeal Squares" was instructed by her grandmother over the years; her conclusion described how making the squares was their special time together. Endings like these take the essay to a new and deeper level, both for the reader and the writer.

Mini-Lesson 3
Ways to Start an Essay

I save this mini-lesson until last in this series because I want students to be finished, or almost finished, with the assignment. If one has a concept of a whole piece, it is easier to find a way into it.

I ask why a first sentence to any piece of writing is important, and most classes can usually come up with many reasons: it gets the reader's attention, it gives a preview for the rest of the piece, it sets the mood, it gives important information, and so on. Students also can generate a partial list of ways to effectively write a first sentence. To their list, I add a few other ideas. In the end, the list looks like this:

Ways To Start an Essay

1. Give a brief anecdote that starts with a sensory detail:

- Crash!

- The blur of blue tiles at the bottom of the pool disappeared as I . . .

- The late afternoon sun slid through the stained glass panels . . .

- The roller coaster screamed against its metal frame as it twisted toward me in the front of the line . . .

2. Create a scenario, using a sensory detail, but beginning with the word "Imagine":

- Imagine the smell of chocolate pudding bubbling on the stove . . .

3. Ask a question.

4. Ask a question using "What if . . ."

5. Give a statement of general truth.

6. Use an interesting statistic.

I explain to the class how a writer could link an introduction and conclusion to frame a piece if she chose to do so. As with conclusions, these introductory techniques are easier to illustrate with actual essays, so I don't exasperate myself trying to explain every single one to its fullest extent. Instead, I wait for opportunities to suggest specific techniques during mini-lessons and individual conferences. Soon, students will become comfortable with a variety of choices. I do, however, tell students how *not* to start an essay in this class: sentences like "I am going to write about . . ." or "One time I went to . . ." are definitely out.

However students start, they should work in the actual topic and main idea(s) by the end of the first paragraph or the beginning of the second. This is important. Readers want to be hooked, but they also want to know up front where the writer is headed.

A Note on Examples

In my examples throughout the year, I try to use writing that is sophisticated but accessible. I want the examples to interest students and inspire them; I want them to think, "Wow, it's good writing, and *I* could do that." I especially try to use strong verbs in my examples, since these are at the heart of effective writing. The verbs, though, are easy ones that students use every day: *slid, screamed, bubbled*. I want students to realize that they already know enough (about words, about life) to write well; with some effort and thought, with mindfulness, they can succeed.

Assignment 2

Process Essay

☐ Read the sample essays and write your answers to the following questions for each essay:

   1. What technique does the author use for an introduction?

   2. Find two sensory details.

   3. Does the author take the conclusion one step further? How?

☐ Think about some activity that you know how to do. It should be something you care about and you think is important. On paper, brainstorm as much as you can about the process and group your ideas.

☐ Add details to your groups—colors, shapes, sounds, smells, textures, tastes.

☐ Write a rough draft. Double space. It should be enough for at least one typed page in the end.

☐ Make sure your conclusion goes the extra step. If you are stuck, try this: Why is this process, hobby, sport, and so on, important? How has it helped you grow? What can a person learn about life through this process?

☐ Look at your beginning. Will the introduction grab the reader's attention? Use your notebook to look for ideas about how to write effective introductions. Is your main idea within the first and second paragraphs?

☐ Read the draft. Ask yourself these questions, and then revise:

   • Are the steps in the proper order?

   • Can I add some transition words (*first, then, next, finally*)?

   • Do I define any words my readers might not understand? Do I give background information?

☐ Try a title. Type up the final copy. Complete an E/R Check Sheet and print your essay.

☐ Clip the E/R Check Sheet, questions, prewriting, rough drafts, the final draft, and this sheet together. Hand in.

		Preliminary Grade	Revised Grade
STRUCTURE (organization, paragraphs, length, font)	20 pts.	_____	_____
PROCESS (questions, brainstorm/groups, rough draft, E/R Check Sheet)	20 pts.	_____	_____
DESCRIPTION (details, banned words, intro, conclusion)	20 pts.	_____	_____
SPELLING	20 pts.	_____	_____
GRAMMAR (punctuation, capitals, sentences, _____)	20 pts.	_____	_____
	TOTAL		_____

How to Make a Holiday Ornament

by Amy MacDonald, eighth grader

Do you have an old, burned-out light bulb at home and want to do more than just throw it away? Here's an idea that will have family and friends in awe of your creativity. At the same time, you will be decorating your Christmas tree.

Ornaments are traditional decorations that look dazzling on your Christmas tree. Instead of buying one at the store, make a fun penguin ornament at home for little or no cost. You will be recycling while having fun! All you need is an old light bulb, acrylic paint in red, black, white, and yellow, a paint brush, ribbon or string, a cotton ball, and glue.

First, dust off or wash the old light bulb, so that nothing gets under the paint or onto you. Lay down newspapers or magazines so that the paint doesn't go onto the table you are working at. Next, paint the entire bulb black (this will become the basic body of the penguin). When the black paint has dried, paint the center to upper part of one side of the bulb white (for the belly and the head). After the white paint is dry, use your creativity to paint on a yellow beak and face. You can also paint on a red bow tie for fun.

After all of the paint for the penguin has completely dried, glue a fluffy cotton ball on top, for the penguin's hat. Then, tie a ribbon around the bulb or poke a hole at the top, and tie the ribbon through that.

Now, you can put your artwork on the Christmas tree and enjoy. Watch as everyone marvels at your fascinating project! If the penguin is looking a little lonely on the tree, make him some friends. Use other light bulbs to make a Santa, snowman, or reindeer ornament to adorn your tree. There are endless possibilities. This is a wonderful way to spend time together as a family, too. Let your creativity out while saving money and helping the environment this season!

How to Do a Lay-up

by Melani Toole, eighth grader

Imagine that you and your basketball team are in the final moments of a tied championship game. You are on a fast break down the court, and there is someone coming right down on you, and your only option is to do a lay-up. You need this winning basket. What would happen if you could only hit outside shots?

Once it is learned, doing a lay-up is one of the easiest ways to score two points in basketball. First, you need to know how to shoot with both your left and right hands. (You don't have to shoot very far, though.) Second, you need to practice how to run down the full court and do a "stop and pop." This means that you go on a fast break and stop a little bit in front of the foul line and pop (shoot).

When those two skills are learned, you are ready to try the lay-up. When you are bringing the ball down the court, and you are going toward the right, you must go further than the foul line, and when you see the last red box (out of four), you look up. As you are going to jump and shoot, there is one important skill to remember. On the right, you must jump off your left foot and bring your right leg up with you. (If you are doing a left lay-up, you jump off your right leg and bring your left leg up with you.) Then you shoot the ball at the hoop. Make sure that you hit the red square on the backboard. You should never "swish" a lay-up. Now you'll be hitting those shots in no time!

Learning this has helped me more than I expected. First, when I couldn't do a lay-up, I never scored any points, or even helped my team out that much. Then, my dad taught me how to do it, and it was so easy that I started teaching other girls that didn't know how. I was so proud of myself for working at it, and getting it down pat. This made me grow as a basketball player and be stronger. I don't mean physically stronger.

I could associate with my teammates when I never could before. Now we talk all the time, and I am very outgoing and willing to help people with skills, or just even introduce myself to a new kid. Once I got through a game with about 16 points just from lay-ups. I have grown to be a better basketball player, and I have much more confidence, too.

CHAPTER 6

Assignment 3
Compare and Contrast Essay

Like the two previous assignments, the Compare and Contrast Essay requires students to use their own experience as material. This serves again as a strong motivator: many a student who claims he doesn't feel like writing is excited to compare and contrast, say, X-Box and PlayStation or two brands of mountain bikes—subjects about which he is knowledgeable and passionate.

During conferences, I help students find topics that suit their interests and expertise. I discourage them from choosing subjects that are completely different or too easy, like "cats and dogs." In that case, I would suggest instead selecting two breeds of dogs, or two actual dogs that the student knows personally. Likewise, if a student wanted to compare and contrast two sports, I would steer her in the direction of two similar sports so she must work with subtleties instead of the obvious. Or, I would help her look for interesting topics within one single sport: instead of comparing and contrasting basketball and lacrosse, the student could concentrate only on basketball and write about two different positions, or two different defense patterns. Whatever the topic, most students need help tightening their focus. I try to instill the habit of looking closely.

Often, I learn quite a bit from these essays. Many times, a student doesn't realize he is an expert at something; he thinks everyone knows how to build three different kinds of birdhouses or tell the

> ## Suggested Mini-Lessons
>
> ❏ 1 COMPARE AND CONTRAST DEFINED; POSSIBLE ORGANIZATION
>
> ❏ 2 CLICHÉS
>
> ❏ 3 TRANSITION WORDS
>
> **Materials:** *Copies of pages 32 and 33 for students.*

difference between a flip turn and open turn in swimming. "Teach me something," I tell them, "I'd love to learn what you know." Sometimes this might mean learning the differences between The Gap and Abercrombie and Fitch at the South Shore Mall. As long as there's sufficient effort in thought and words, I'll keep an open mind.

In this assignment we take the idea of essay structure one step further. The Process Essay required only a basic, linear format. Now, students get two new structural methods to choose from. This is an extremely important lesson: students can see that writers make choices not only about content but also about organization. In addition, having students conceptualize the same ideas in two different arrangements exercises the mind and opens up pathways for future writing.

I remind the class that sensory details must be included and banned words avoided. I also remind students that they should refer to their notes about introductions and conclusions from the last assignment. They are expected to have strong beginnings and endings for every assignment now, and their grades will reflect that. I encourage them to try different techniques than they used for the Process Essay; during individual conferences I make more specific suggestions. One concluding technique that works well for this genre is to give a personal opinion about the two subjects. This puts a fresh twist on the end of the essay, and provides a chance to reiterate some of the main points. Students who are comparing two objects (as opposed to people or places) can give the ending a "consumer report" tone: which would they recommend to potential buyers and why? When I confer with a student, I help her imagine more than one introduction or conclusion for her essay, and even jot down the ideas in the corner of her rough draft, so that she can think about it on her own and choose what she likes best.

Mini-Lesson 1
Compare and Contrast Defined; Possible Organization

Many eighth graders don't realize that *compare* and *contrast* have two different meanings. When asked to think about it, they remember that *contrast* means differentiate; by elimination, then, they see that to *compare* is to liken. I stress to them that on tests, standardized or otherwise, they should only do what is asked: if the directions ask only for a comparison, they need not additionally contrast.

I give students their two options for structure: by topic or by characteristic. On the board, I list the formats for each:

TOPIC

1. Introduction
2. Topic 1: all characteristics
3. Topic 2: all characteristics
4. Conclusion

BY CHARACTERISTIC

1. Introduction
2. Characteristic 1: both topics
3. Characteristic 2: both topics
4. Characteristic 3: both topics
5. Conclusion

Each number represents a paragraph. To middle school students, then, the By Topic method is clearly the better choice, since there are fewer paragraphs to write. Not so, I tell them: the same amount of writing goes into each technique; though the By Topic method has fewer paragraphs, the paragraphs are longer. Of course,

students who choose to write by characteristic can have as many "characteristic" paragraphs as they want; three is only a minimum. Sometimes a student will invent a subtle organizational variation on these two structures. I welcome this as long as it makes sense and I feel confident that the student knows what he's doing.

Beside the lists I note an example that most students will understand; sometimes I give two. The easiest examples involve school issues, like block scheduling and short-class scheduling, the new library and the old, or seventh grade and eighth grade. I demonstrate how to formulate "characteristic" paragraphs for the second structural method. For example, in a potential essay about the new library and the old, instead of writing a tiny paragraph only about "computers," I advise writing a paragraph about "technology" which would include not only computers but also the new DVD player and computerized book catalogue. Hometown sports examples are always of more interest, to both boys and girls. I've used Red Sox managers, Patriots quarterbacks, and new and old stadiums. Finally, I verbally model introductions and conclusions for the imaginary essays. Students are then ready to begin writing.

Mini-Lesson 2
Clichés

I continue my discussion about language. This mini-lesson is strategically placed in line with the mini-lessons about banned words, sensory details. Clichés are cousins to banned words: they are so overused that their meanings are powerless. They do not offer the reader anything fresh, exciting, thought-provoking, or precise. Our job as writers, I reiterate to students, is to communicate our thoughts in a clear, interesting way.

Clichés can be problematic for middle school students because they are difficult to define. Clichés can be words, phrases, sayings, similes, and so on. But of course not all words, phrases, sayings, and similes are clichés. A word can be a cliché in one situation but meaningful in another. It is much easier to ban words completely than to uproot clichés on a case-by-case basis! For most students, recognizing clichés takes time and training: often they don't even realize that certain phrases and words are overused. To them, using a cliché like "give it my best shot" is like using the word "pencil": you wouldn't call a pencil anything else, would you? Likewise, many students can't imagine that alternatives to clichés even exist.

Here are some clichés that serve as useful examples:

as cold as ice

you are what you eat

word of mouth

home is where the heart is

seize the day

the grass is always greener

warm welcome

in the blink of an eye

free as a bird

I let students add to this list; often I have to end the mini-lesson with hands waving in the air. "Whatever you're thinking," I tell them, "don't use it in your writing."

I usually don't try to explain that ideas can be clichéd, too. Students have enough to process with linguistic clichés. But as the year progresses, I push students during individual conferences to think beyond clichéd topics. Although it is more difficult, I assure them, the path of looking closely is always more rewarding.

Mini-Lesson 3 Transition Words

When writing the Process Essay, students used words like *first, second, third, then, next, finally,* and so on. With the Compare and Contrast Essay, students advance to a new level of transition words. I save this mini-lesson for last in the series because transition words can be easily appended to a nearly finished piece. Useful transition words for this type of essay include those listed below.

I keep these lists on posters so students can refer to them all year. I encourage them to try any of the words at any time; I'll help them with adjustments. For this assignment, they will need to use at least four of these words. For future assignments, no exact numbers of transition words are required, but I will subtract points when the lack of a transition leaves a hole in the flow of the piece. During conferences, I advocate for transition words: pointing to a certain place in the writing, I affirm, "This is a perfect spot for a transition word. Look at the poster. Which one do you think would work here?" When the student chooses one that fits, I respond, "Excellent. Now that sentence is really polished."

ADDING IDEAS	CONTRASTING IDEAS	COMPARING IDEAS	CONCLUSIONS
in addition	in/by contrast	likewise	thus
plus	however	similarly	hence
moreover	yet	in the same way	therefore
furthermore	conversely		
also	on the contrary		
	on the other hand		
	although		

Name _____ Date _____ Period _____

Assignment 3

Compare and Contrast Essay

❏ Read the two sample essays and write your answers to the following questions for each essay:

    1. What organizational technique did the writer use?

    2. What technique did the writer use for an introduction?

    3. What technique did the writer use for a conclusion?

    4. What are three transition words used in the piece?

❏ Choose two topics (people, places, objects, animals, sports, and on so on) to compare and contrast. Choose topics you are interested in and know a lot about. Look through your Topics for Writing for ideas.

❏ On paper, prewrite your ideas:

    1. Brainstorm a list for each topic.

    2. Decide which organizational technique you will use.

    3. Group your ideas into paragraphs.

❏ Write a first draft. Review your notes for introduction and conclusion techniques.

❏ Revise the draft. Check for the following:

    _____ a title   _____ an attention-grabbing introduction

    _____ a strong conclusion   _____ at least four transition words

❏ Type the draft if you have not already. The final copy should be at least one typed page.

❏ Complete an E/R Check Sheet. Hand in questions, prewriting, rough draft(s), final copy, E/R Check Sheet, and this sheet.

		Preliminary Grade	Revised Grade
STRUCTURE (organization, paragraphs, length, font)	20 pts.	_____	_____
PROCESS (questions, brainstorm/groups, rough draft, E/R Check Sheet)	20 pts.	_____	_____
DESCRIPTION (intro, conclusion, banned words, clichés, transition words)	20 pts.	_____	_____
SPELLING	20 pts.	_____	_____
GRAMMAR (punctuation, capitals, sentences, _____)	20 pts.	_____	_____
	TOTAL		_____

Middle School: A Different World

by Amy MacDonald, eighth grader

Imagine changing your setting from a laid-back smaller environment to a fast-paced larger one. When I entered East Middle School, I had no idea what a different world it would be from my sheltered elementary school.

Morrison Elementary School had been my educational setting for five years of my life. The two-floor school had surrounded me with dramatically different age groups, children varying from grade one to grade five. By contrast, East Middle School has only three different grades, one grade on each of its three floors. The variation among students is not as noticeable as it was at Morrison. At Morrison, the age difference brought each grade closer together. At East, there seems to be so many more faces. In addition, students from all of east Braintree go here—not just the former pupils from Morrison.

Morrison shielded students quite a bit, and did not expect too much from us. However, we also were not given many privileges. We would always have to walk in straight lines down the hallways with the teacher leading. We had to be told when we could go to the bathroom as well. At East, students are freer. We can walk down the hall alone, go to the bathroom when we want, and basically hold it upon ourselves to follow the rules. Because of the numerous privileges we have, we also have more responsibilities. Pupils always need to be prepared for class and arrive on time. We are treated more like adults, but we are expected to behave like adults would as well. Also, students are punished more if they do not live up to their responsibilities.

Although Morrison and East are very different, the overall goals of both schools are the same, and each succeeds in attaining these goals. Both schools have a wonderful learning environment and excellent teachers. Moreover, at both schools students have to work for their grades. Finally, at both schools students enjoy the safe, fun and challenging atmosphere.

This is now my third year at East Middle School, and I have adjusted to all of the changes by now. I guess this is an example of how as fish get older, they have to go to a bigger pond. As I get older, I will need to adapt to new difficulties, and going to an even larger, more challenging school is one of them. I can only imagine the differences I will see next year at the high school.

What's Wrong with Braintree's Park?

by Alex Cerri, eighth grader

The roar of wheels and slap of skateboards are familiar sounds at any skate park. But are all skate parks the same? To the untrained eye, Skaters Island in Rhode Island and the Braintree Skate Park may seem very similar. In reality, drastic differences leave Braintree's skate park struggling and Skaters Island prospering.

The atmospheres of both parks are extremely different. Skaters Island is a massive, 25,000 square-foot indoor skate park. It has a smooth linoleum–like floor, and Skatelite™ ramps. Braintree's park, however, is a badly designed outdoor concrete and asphalt skate park. Skaters Island has music playing at all times, giving you something to skate to, to keep your adrenaline flowing. There are colorful banners on the walls as well. Braintree Skate Park has almost the exact opposite. It is full of bland gray concrete ramps on a black asphalt round. Even on the most crowded days, it feels devoid of life.

The features of the parks differ as well. Skaters Island has a huge, flowing, wooden bowl, and an insane half-pipe. There is also a snake run. It is very well designed; you can get speed, and maintain it, something very rare in other skate parks' ramps. It has flowing hips, tight turns, and high banks, all perfect for carving. Braintree's park, on the other hand, is almost the complete opposite. The ramps have tight transition, robbing speed from the skater. The designers forgot the most important aspect of a skate park: flow. It is almost impossible to get speed anywhere in the park without vigorous pushing. And while Skaters Island has almost 40 ramps, Braintree's park has a mere nine ramps, two of which shouldn't even be counted as ramps since they are small concrete bumps.

The only characteristic where the Braintree Skate Park surpasses Skaters Island is in the people who frequent the park. I know the people at Braintree's park like friends, since I see them so often. They help and encourage me, and I do the same for them. By contrast, Skaters Island has an unknown, mysterious, sometimes ornery crowd. In addition, it is sometimes very crowded. I could stand at the lip of a bowl for 15 minutes, waiting for my 2 minute run.

Skaters Island is by far the better skate park. It was made by skaters, for skaters. Although it costs thirteen dollars for admission, it is well worth it. Braintree Skate Park is sloppily put together. The designers missed what a skate park should be. Instead of making an innovative creative outlet for skaters, they made what they, a group of non-skaters, thought would be a sufficient park.

CHAPTER 7

Assignment 4
Persuasive Essay

Many students will give their Compare and Contrast Essays a persuasive slant. This, combined with the fact that most middle school students like to debate and are full of opinions, makes for a smooth transition to the Persuasive Essay. I spend a mini-lesson discussing the definition of *persuasion* and some possible topics. I also give the class a basic six-paragraph formula for setting up a persuasive essay. I teach a traditional format because most of the students have never learned one; therefore, it is a useful place to start. In subsequent assignments, I encourage students to experiment with other structures that make sense to them. For now, though, I want the fundamentals secure in their minds.

I keep a World Almanac in my room for reference; many students consult it during this assignment, looking for statistics that can back up their claims. In addition, I allow students to use the library and Internet for research if they request to do so.

Suggested Mini-Lessons

☐ 1 PERSUASION INTRODUCED; POTENTIAL TOPICS; ORGANIZATION

☐ 2 TITLES

☐ 3 STRONG VERBS

Materials: Copies of pages 38 and 39 for students.

Mini-Lesson 1
Persuasion Introduced; Potential Topics; Organization

Most students know the meaning of the word *persuade*. If they think through their day, they will realize how often they use persuasion: when trying to convince their parents to let them go out with friends; when offering to wash an older sibling's car if he would drive them to the mall; when begging a teacher to postpone a test. In a persuasive essay, the writer tries to convince the reader that her view on an issue is the better view. The first step for the student is to find an opinion to which he feels connected. We review the difference between fact and opinion, and for some classes I hand out ten statements that students must label as fact or opinion. An opinion, I explain, is the main idea; facts can be used only to back

it up. I tell students to ask themselves after they have chosen topics, "Could somebody argue the other side?" If the answer is yes, they have chosen an opinion.

In addition, I stress to the students that their opinions should be ones that other normal minds would debate. For example, arguing that legislators should uphold the law prohibiting people to drive on the wrong side of the road would be a terrible topic. No sane person would disagree with that opinion. An essay about raising the legal driving age from 16 to 18, however, would draw strong reactions, whether pro or con, from most readers. I encourage students to search their Topics for Writing, looking for anything that might lend itself to an interesting, debatable opinion. For students who claim they've drawn a blank, I offer a pretyped list of general topic areas that might help. I've included a version of this list in Appendix C. Sometimes, a topic from the list will resonate with a student; sometimes a topic from the list will remind a student of another topic from her own experience. Some students know right away what they feel strongly about. Of course, some students will claim that they have no ideas whatsoever; I will then spend our conferencing time probing their interests, hobbies, and daily life until we hit upon something that sparks an opinion. Finally, I emphasize to students that they must clearly choose a side of a given argument; they should not choose topics about which they are lukewarm. Arguing both sides of a topic without a clear preference will only confuse the reader and annoy a state test grader.

On the board, I list a traditional way to set up a persuasive essay:

> Paragraph 1:
>   Introduction
>
> Paragraph 2:
>   Reason #1 with examples, statistics, illustrations, and so on
>
> Paragraph 3:
>   Reason #2 with examples, statistics, illustrations, and so on
>
> Paragraph 4:
>   Reason #3 with examples, statistics, illustrations, and so on
>
> Paragraph 5:
>   The other side's view, and why they're wrong
>
> Paragraph 6:
>   Conclusion

I encourage students to brainstorm as much as they can about the topic, and then to group their ideas into "reason" paragraphs. As always, ideas can be cut or added at any time. A minimum of three reasons will build an effective argument; one could always have more than three, adding paragraphs to the middle of the essay. I remind students that once the reason groups are formed, they should add examples and even do a bit of research if applicable. For the paragraph about the other side's view, I suggest that using the phrase "Some people think . . ." is an easy way to start. Students can finish that

thought with some aspect of the opposite view and then explain why that viewpoint is wrong, using a transition word like "however": "Some people think that it is more convenient for 16- and 17-year-olds to be able to drive themselves around, instead of having other people drive them everywhere until their eighteenth birthday. However, safety is always more important than convenience." (I try to illustrate with topics students would never choose.) A separate paragraph about the other side's view may be unnecessary if the writer has addressed the opposite viewpoint throughout the essay.

Finally, I remind students that strong introductions and conclusions are especially important in a persuasive essay. In the introductory paragraph, the writer should clarify his position after getting the reader's attention. If he wants, he can give a taste of his reasons, but only a taste. One conclusion technique that could work well for this assignment is to come up with a solution to the problem. This may not apply to all topics, so students should consult their notebooks and use their best judgments. A powerful last sentence might have an "if . . . then" construction: "If you agree that humans need trees to live, then you will join me in writing to lawmakers to minimize deforestation." A question is perhaps the strongest ending of all: "What would become of us if we robbed ourselves of our own oxygen supply by killing all the trees?"

Mini-Lesson 2
Titles

Until now, I have required students to title their essays, but I have not emphasized it. I explain that as with everything else, inventing a strong title is a technique that can be practiced. In their notebooks, students brainstorm a list of what an effective title should do. I suggest that they think of their favorite book, story, poem, or movie and think about its title. Is the title effective? If so, what about it makes it good? We generate a class list on the board:

EFFECTIVE TITLES:

⋄ get a reader's attention

⋄ tell something about the topic

⋄ are interesting

⋄ make you want to read the rest

⋄ make you curious

To this I add the idea that titles sometimes have a double meaning, which makes the reader stop and think after she has read the work. One clear illustration of this is S. E. Hinton's *The Outsiders*, which we have in our seventh-grade curriculum. I ask students, what does Hinton's title mean? Who are the outsiders? What are they outside of? When students start to think about it, they realize that more characters than just the Greasers can be considered "outsiders." This twist, I emphasize, relates to the book's theme. A title, then, can point to some deeper meaning of the work it names.

This discussion helps students understand the nature of effective titles, but it doesn't necessarily make them feel any more confident about writing one. That's okay, I tell them; as with all difficult skills, it takes time to practice. I encourage them to be patient with themselves and try their best. Like introductions, titles are best dealt with after the entire piece is written. If something pops into their mind while writing, they should jot it down, but they needn't think too much about it until the end. During conferences, I can give students more specific guidance.

Mini-Lesson 3
Strong Verbs

I continue my discourse on removing the weak parts of one's writing and adding more punch. Verbs, I declare, are the heart of the sentence. As writers, we must try to use the most specific verbs possible. The good news, I tell students, is that they already know enough strong verbs; they don't have to study the dictionary! They need only think and look closely.

I put a few sentences on the board:

> As I went down the street, I saw him from the corner of my eye. I knew he was the one who beat up my little brother. I was nervous. Should I go up to him? I decided I would, and I turned quickly and went toward him.

I have students copy the paragraph in their notebooks and underline all the verbs. (It may be necessary to review the definition of *verb*.) I ask them to think of any better replacements for the underlined verbs and to write them in. Most students will recognize the first verb, "went," as rather flat and will replace it with "walked." Better, I tell them, but are there any other verbs that are even more descriptive than "walked?" I suggest visualizing the person walking. How is he or she walking? We generate a short list of "words instead of *walk*" beside the paragraph. It usually includes terms like *strolled, sauntered, skipped, strode* and *strutted*. If this were your piece of writing, I tell students, you could now choose the verb that best fits your meaning. I then remind them that to "see someone from the corner of your eye" is a bit of a cliché; is there a verb or verb phrase that could replace the whole phrase? We note verbs like *glimpsed, spied,* and *spotted*. How about "beat up," I ask. I warn students to always question two-part verbs, that is, verbs that have a preposition attached to them. Sometimes they can't be avoided, but many times they are replaceable. Students offer words like *pummeled, attacked, walloped,* and *pounded*. Some students will then spot "go up" as a two-part verb, and replace it with *approach, confront, face,* and *challenge*. The other trick, I advise, is to change verbs that pair with an adverb, like "turn quickly." Can we eliminate the adverb with a more precise verb? Students realize that *spun* or *whirled* might be better.

Finally, I tell the class about the archenemy of strong verbs: the word *is* in all its forms (*am, are, was, were*). To answer their puzzled looks, I explain: *is* by itself (that is, not followed by an *-ing* word) is a linking verb that has no action. Sometimes I illustrate this by writing different verbs, both active and linking, each on its own index card, and inviting students to perform the action on the card they are given. Students who receive cards with action verbs must dance, sing, twirl, hop, and so on, to the delight of the class.

Students who receive cards with linking verbs just shrug and stand there, to the class's disappointment. That's what it feels like in writing as well, I tell them. If writers use too many sentences without action, the piece starts to feel dry and boring. Try to use only one linking verb per paragraph. Do you see any in this paragraph, I ask? Students spot two. The first can stay, I tell them, but what about the second? Students immediately offer the word *felt*, which is slightly better sounding than "was," but technically still a linking verb. Try this, I suggest: take the most important part of the sentence, and try to attach it to another sentence either before or after. We agree that "nervous" should be salvaged, and we attach it to the following sentence. The revised paragraph might sound like this:

> As I strolled down the street, I glimpsed him to my right. I knew he was the one who pummeled my little brother. Nervous, I wondered if I should confront him. I decided I would, spun on my heel, and strode toward him.

I stress to students that we used verbs that they already knew. For this assignment, students will have to find five verbs to replace, and they should clearly show the revisions on their rough drafts. If a student asks to use a thesaurus, I discourage him for now: though the thesaurus is a convenient and helpful tool, I want students to become self-sufficient, since thesauruses are not permitted during our state's test. At another time during the year, I will explain how to use a thesaurus. For now, I spend conferencing time helping students locate and replace weak verbs.

Ways to Strengthen Verbs

1. Visualize the action clearly and try to think of a more specific word.

2. Try to replace two-part verbs (verbs that have a preposition attached to them).

3. Try to replace verbs that need an adverb. Is there one word that could say both?

4. Try to limit *is, am, was,* and *were* to one per paragraph. You may need to rearrange sentences.

Assignment 4

Persuasive Essay

☐ Read the two sample essays and write your answers to the following questions for each essay:

   1. What does the author do for an introduction?

   2. What side of this issue is the author on?

   3. In your opinion, which of the author's reasons is the strongest?

   4. What is the other side's view?

   5. What technique is used in the conclusion?

☐ Choose a topic to write about and brainstorm some of your ideas on paper. Organize your ideas into paragraph groups. Make sure to have a paragraph about the other side's view.

☐ Write a rough draft. Use your notebook for help with the introduction and conclusion.

☐ Read the essay. Revise. Make sure you have the following:

   _____ an interesting title   _____ an attention-grabbing introduction

   _____ supporting evidence for each reason   _____ examples and sensory details

   _____ the other side's view   _____ transition words

   _____ a strong conclusion

☐ Go through the essay once more and underline five weak verbs. Change them to stronger ones.

☐ Type up the final copy. It should be at least one typed page.

☐ Complete an E/R Check Sheet. Hand in questions, prewriting, rough draft(s), final copy, E/R Check Sheet, and this sheet.

		Preliminary Grade	Revised Grade
STRUCTURE (organization, paragraphs, length, font)	20 pts.	_____	_____
PROCESS (questions, brainstorm/group, rough, E/R Check Sheet)	20 pts.	_____	_____
DESCRIPTION (title, intro, conclusion, examples, banned words, strong verbs, transition words)	20 pts.	_____	_____
SPELLING	20 pts.	_____	_____
GRAMMAR (punctuation, capitals, sentences, _____)	20 pts.	_____	_____
	TOTAL		_____

PERSUASIVE ESSAY SAMPLES

Lower the Working Age

by Samantha White, eighth grader

Imagine your seventh- or eighth-grade child carefully bagging groceries at the supermarket, smiling and talking to all the busy people shopping. Your child is learning how to be polite, and learning responsibility. However, children cannot get a job until they are fourteen. They can't earn their own money and experience real life until that age. In my opinion, the working age should be twelve or thirteen.

If a child could work at twelve or thirteen, he would have some extra spending money for when he wants to go to the movies or the mall. If a child has a job, she wouldn't be constantly bugging her parents to give out money. The child would be able to have her own pocket change.

The job doesn't have to be a difficult one. The child could be a bus boy at a restaurant, or bag groceries at a supermarket. She could do anything within her capability. In addition, the working hours don't have to be long. Just a couple hours a week could teach the child responsibility and give him more confidence.

Furthermore, the children who have jobs at a younger age would be less likely to get into trouble. For example, some thirteen-year-olds may want to go out drinking with friends on Friday night. The child that has a job obviously isn't going to be drinking. Having a job can keep children safe.

Some people think that if children under fourteen have jobs, it would be unhealthy. They think it would shorten the child's childhood. However, having a job would not be mandatory. Children under fourteen can choose if they want to work or not.

To protect children, there could be a legal amount of hours a child under fourteen could work. There could also be a law saying that any child under fourteen cannot work past 9:00 PM. I know that working at twelve or thirteen is only a one or two year difference. But even that one year can make a positive change.

Should Public Schools Get Uniforms?

by Kayla Hall, eighth grader

Picture a school where all students are equal. Kids walk the halls without the worry of being made fun of because of their outer appearance. This may sound like just a fantasy, but in fact, it could become a reality in every school across the nation. Having uniforms in public schools could make this dream come true.

Sadly, teens often judge others by what they wear. Every day, kids are tormented by their peers for wearing clothes that are considered "not cool." This major problem could be easily solved if all kids wore uniforms to school. If everyone was dressed exactly the same, then no one could judge others by what they wear. Kids would take the time to get to know each other, instead of saying, "I don't like her clothes, so obviously she isn't good enough to be friends with me." With uniforms, teens would decide whether they like someone or not based on personality alone.

In addition, wearing uniforms would save kids the stress of deciding what to wear to school every day. Kids spend more time figuring out what to wear than they spend actually getting ready for school. Kids are often late for school as a result of this. If kids were required to wear uniforms to school every day, then they wouldn't have to spend time and energy worrying about what to wear.

Moreover, since kids would feel more comfortable in their school surroundings if they wore uniforms, they would do better in school. The thought of being ridiculed for the way you look is often terrifying. Kids could walk down the school hallways wearing uniforms with confidence.

Many parents and kids argue that kids should be able to express their individuality through clothes. However, there are many other ways of expressing one's individuality than through fashion. Kids need to learn that inner beauty is far more important than outer beauty. Furthermore, instead of demonstrating individuality, clothes often stereotype kids as preps, goths, geeks, skaters, and so on.

Having uniforms would make a school a safer and friendlier environment. It would end a lot of prejudice among kids, lower their stress levels, and make them do better in school. A possible compromise may be to have four days of school during which students wear uniforms and then a day of free style. If all public schools made uniforms a requirement, they would also make the world of education a better place.

CHAPTER 8

Assignment 5
Letter for Social Change

This assignment demonstrates that writing well is not just a skill or hobby; it can be a tool for positive change. At first, students are surprised to discover that they will actually mail these letters; soon, however, disbelief yields to excitement as we explore topics and students realize that their voices will be heard somewhere in the world.

The letter will be a persuasive essay. I give students a list of potential recipients and their related topics. We discuss the meaning of "social change" and how this principle will affect their topic choices. Students must believe that their argument is for the benefit of society and is not just a gripe about a personal annoyance. Students may not use the same topic they wrote about in the previous assignment; they must start anew. Some students are disappointed, but most can find something else that inspires them. Sometimes, a student will formulate an argument that should be sent to someone outside the list. I help the student locate an appropriate recipient, using the Internet or a phone book.

I supply business envelopes, but I don't provide stamps. If your school will supply them, wonderful. If you can afford stamps yourself, terrific. Since I can have more than 100 letter writers, I give students the choice of bringing in a stamp from home or buying one from me. I slip in a few freebees for students who I know need them. Then, once students get a final grade, they print a fresh copy of the letter in single space, seal it in the envelope, and give it to me. I deposit the letters in the school's mailbox.

> ## Suggested Mini-Lessons
>
> ❏ 1 EXPLANATION OF LETTER; TOPICS AND ADDRESSES; ENVELOPES
>
> ❏ 2 AUDIENCE
>
> ❏ 3 SENTENCE VARIATION
>
> **Materials:** Copies of pages 44–47 for students.

I record what letters have actually been sent and inform students that the grades of unsent letters will not count. I want them to follow through on this assignment; I want them to feel what their writing can do.

The responses to the letters vary. Most letters sent to public officials are read by aides who send a form letter in response. Some students receive whole packets of pictures and other paraphernalia. Other letters sent to smaller offices, like those of our Town Council or our principal, receive personal responses. With a few phone calls, I try to convince whomever I can to help out; most small-office elected officials are happy to oblige, since the votes from students' parents are important to them. Every year, at least one student gets a personal reply from a larger office. One year a student got a personal letter from the governor thanking her for sending her views. Another year a student received a short note from one of the governor's aides asking him to call to further discuss his ideas. The student called after school and chatted with the aide for about ten minutes, long enough to instill a lifelong memory; he was elated for weeks. (The aide couldn't have picked a better person to connect with, since the student had wanted to study politics even before writing the letter.)

I explain to all students that they could get this kind of response but that even if they don't, they should not be discouraged by a form-letter reply. It's physically impossible for a president, senator, congressperson, or governor to focus on all of his or her work and still have time to write back to everyone. And we don't *want* them spending all of their time and our money writing letters. The aides have the time to read, record, and respond to letters. (I emphasize "record.") The aides then inform their bosses of the topics and opinions coming in. I stress to students that letters, phone calls, and e-mails about issues they care about are never a waste of effort: when public officials vote on an issue, they check the number of letters and phone calls from their constituents and factor those into their decisions. If students want to change something in the world around them, I suggest, they should become active with their voice.

Mini-Lesson 1
Explanation of Letter; Topics and Addresses; Envelopes

Students easily understand the task: write a persuasive essay to a specific person. Some students will choose a topic and recipient immediately, and some will need to peruse the address list a while. We read through the list as a class so that I can answer any questions. I have included a skeleton list in this chapter; each reader should fill in the appropriate names and any additional corresponding topics. I give the classes my pep talk about the importance of using one's voice for positive change, and assure students that nearly all of them will receive a response.

I direct students to simply put a persuasive essay in letter format. (Most should remember how to set up a letter from our first assignment. I refer any who don't to the example on page 23.) I remind students to leave space for their signatures in the closing; when they actually sign the letter they experience feelings of authority and ownership.

I diagram an addressed envelope on the board and students copy it into their notebooks. In my first year teaching this assignment, I did not think this would be necessary; I was wrong. I also take ten seconds to demonstrate the tri-fold method of folding a letter. Doing this eliminates envelopes with thick wads of paper in their corners. Finally, I remind students not to put the letters in the envelopes until all revisions are made and they have received a final grade. At that time, they can print a fresh single-spaced copy to be mailed. Students are now ready to begin writing.

Mini-Lesson 2
Audience

Students know what an audience is. When asked to apply the idea to writing, they quickly realize that the audience is "the person who reads the writing." In addition, I tell them that the audience is the *intended* reader that the author writes to; the audience for a piece of writing already exists in the author's mind long before anyone has read the work.

I ask students to consider our first assignment, the Introductory Letter: "Who was the audience for that?" I ask them. Cleary it was me. But what about the Persuasive Essay? I have students ask themselves whom they imagined as their audience. Perhaps it was me, perhaps their parents, perhaps all adults in general, perhaps kids their own age. I list the groups on the board as students answer. I then ask the following questions:

YOUNG CHILDREN	YOUR AGE	ADULTS
easy to understand	bigger words	difficult
pictures	fewer or no pictures	no pictures
big writing	medium writing	small writing
easy plots	more involved	complicated
about right and wrong	characters have tough decisions	even tougher choices

- Think of the novels in your English class. Are you the target audience? How do you know?
- Think of the books, newspapers, or magazines you've seen your parents (or other adults) read. Would you enjoy reading them? Why or why not?
- Think of your social studies textbook. Was it written for kids? How do you know? What do you imagine a college history textbook to be like?

It is helpful to chart the differences. I use books as examples, but television shows, movies, or music will also work. I list some potential audiences and solicit characteristics.

There are an almost infinite number of audiences, I add: people of different genders, races, cultures, religions, geographic areas, and areas of interest and expertise. Writers constantly think about whom they write for. This is especially true when persuading. I advise students to imagine their target audience when writing this letter. How will they react? I tell students to let this information guide their tone of voice, the facts and examples they include, their solution to the problem, and so on. Just as an author of books for small children would never use college-level vocabulary words, students should not write to the principal the way they would write a note to a friend.

Students and I will revisit the idea of audience before the standardized test date; for now, I seek to cultivate an awareness.

Mini-Lesson 3
Sentence Variation

By now, some students will have already heard this lesson from me during individual conferences. I explain to the class that all sentences have a certain form, and using the same form too often in one paragraph gets boring and repetitive.

A pitcher wouldn't throw the same pitch ten times in a row, would he? I ask why not, and get a variety of answers: "Because the hitter would know what's coming." "Because the fans would be bored." "Because everyone would think he doesn't know what else to do." Exactly, I reply. It's the same with writing.

I once attended a staff development conference led by Mitzi Merrill, who summed it up in one simple rule that went something like this: "Don't start two sentences in a row the same way." She meant it literally: don't use the same words twice. This seems easy enough for eighth graders to grasp, without my having to delve into a lengthy grammar lesson on clauses or subject placement. I therefore extend the rule as follows: "Don't start two sentences in the same paragraph the same way." If a sentence starts with "There are," then the student should avoid that phrasing for the remainder of the paragraph. I put an example on the board:

Many people die from smoking each year. Many people leave behind children and spouses.

Students copy it into their notebooks, and work on changing one of the sentences. They realize it is not that difficult. Answers include:

Smoking kills thousands each year. Many people leave behind children and spouses.

Each year, many people die from smoking, and they leave behind children and spouses.

Sadly, many people die from smoking each year, leaving behind children and spouses.

I list some helpful tips on the board:

WAYS TO VARY YOUR SENTENCES

1. Change the duplicated words to other words with the same meaning.

2. Rephrase the whole sentence.

3. Combine the sentences to eliminate the repetitive words.

4. Flip the sentence around: use the second half as the first half.

5. Try a transition word.

6. Try a prepositional phrase.

7. Try an adverb.

It doesn't take much, I assure them, but it will make a big difference.

Name _____ Date _____ Period _____

 Assignment 5
Letter for Social Change

❏ Read the two sample letters and write your answers to the following questions for each letter:

    1. What technique is used for the introduction?

    2. In your opinion, what is the author's strongest reason?

    3. What is the other side's view?

    4. What technique is used for the conclusion?

    5. Find three transition words or phrases and list them.

❏ Review the address sheet and choose your audience—that is, the person who will receive your letter. If you cannot find the right recipient for your argument, see me for help.

❏ On paper, brainstorm ideas about your topic, and group them into reason paragraphs. Be sure to have a paragraph about the other side's view.

❏ Write a rough draft, setting up the essay as a letter.

❏ Read the letter. Revise. Make sure you have the following:

_____ an attention-grabbing introduction	_____ supporting evidence for each reason
_____ examples and sensory details	_____ the other side's view
_____ transition words	_____ a strong conclusion
_____ closing and signature	_____ your address, recipient's address, date

❏ Skim your letter again to make sure no two sentences start the same way in any paragraph. Make changes as needed.

❏ Find four weak verbs and change them to stronger ones.

❏ Type up a final copy if you have not done so already. The paragraphs should add up to at least one typed page. Double space for now.

❏ Complete an E/R Check Sheet. Hand in questions, prewriting, rough draft(s), final copy, this sheet, and E/R Check Sheet.

		Preliminary Grade	Revised Grade
STRUCTURE (letter format, paragraphs, length, font)	20 pts.	_____	_____
PROCESS (questions, brainstorm/group, rough, E/R Check Sheet)	20 pts.	_____	_____
DESCRIPTION (title, intro, conclusion, examples, banned words, verbs, transition words, sentence variation)	20 pts.	_____	_____
SPELLING	20 pts.	_____	_____
GRAMMAR (punctuation, capitals, sentences, _____)	20 pts.	_____	_____
	TOTAL		_____

ADDRESSES FOR LETTER 🍎 FOR SOCIAL CHANGE

CONTACT PERSON	RELEVANT TOPICS
President _____ The White House 1600 Pennsylvania Ave NW Washington DC 20500	national issues, environmental issues, war, education, foreign policy, homeland security, taxes, nationwide laws, employment
First Lady/Gentleman _____ (use same address as above)	(will vary with individual)
Congressman/woman _____	state issues, state environment issues, state/national education, statewide programs, national laws
Senator _____	state issues, state environment issues, state/national education, statewide programs, national laws
Governor _____	state issues, public transportation, state education, state taxes, state environmental issues
Mayor _____	city issues, city taxes, your town's streets and sidewalks, trash pick-up, snow removal, streetlights, parks
Principal _____	any school issue
Letters to the Editor _____	any issue you want to argue to the general public and that is appropriate or relevant to the public

SOME SOCIAL CHANGE GENERAL TOPICS

Environment	Employment	Driving	People	Education
• deforestation • waste management • emissions control • pollution • green space	• jobless rate • minimum wage • working hours • working age	• driving age • cell phones • seatbelts • punishments for law-breakers	• homelessness • prison system • capital punishment	• state/national standardized testing • after-school programs • class sizes • school building conditions • school materials • school schedules

52 Stonegate Drive
Braintree, MA 02184

January 30, 2003

Mr. Joseph Powers
Town Clerk
Braintree Town Hall
One John Fitzgerald Kennedy Memorial Drive
Braintree, MA 02184

Dear Mr. Powers,

Imagine arriving to school early but receiving a detention for being late to homeroom because at your locker, you couldn't find your books easily enough and cram your coat fast enough. Lockers have always been a problem in middle schools. They are much too small to fit everything inside. Our schools should have bigger and better lockers.

With the lockers the size that they are, kids have trouble keeping themselves organized. Our school has to have locker clean-outs almost every month. When it comes time to go home, it takes us forever to find the books that we need. We end up late for the bus, and aggravate our parents for not arriving home on time.

At our school, if a student is late to class, he has to have a late pass to keep himself out of detention. In between classes, we have to go to our lockers to get out our books for the next class. Because of the locker chaos, we arrive late for class without a pass. That gives us nothing but a front seat in detention, just because we couldn't find our books in our tiny lockers.

The size of our lockers not only affects the school's belongings, but it affects our personal belongings as well. Every day when I go home, I get in trouble with my mom for bringing home a dirty coat. I've even come home with my brand new white coat ripped. She wasn't too happy when that happened.

I understand that you don't want to spend all of the town's money on new lockers for middle school students. However, you would actually be saving money by getting new lockers because the school's supplies would not be ruined. In addition, you would save teachers the aggravation of assigning detentions.

Please consider my request. If you want to improve the lives of students, teachers, and parents, then you will agree that new lockers are necessary.

Sincerely,

Jillian Allington

16 Terrace Street
Dorchester, MA 02122

March 7, 2003

Governor Mitt Romney
State House
Office of the Governor
Room 360
Boston, MA 02133

Dear Governor Romney,

Adults are constantly trying to find a solution to the problem of why some students do so poorly in school. I think that having statewide after-school programs could solve this issue. The programs could focus on academics and state testing, or even on crafts.

After-school programs would keep kids busy after school. Attending after-school programs would help students put their academics above watching television or wasting time with friends. In addition, it would help kids get their homework done, which would improve their grades.

For awhile now I have been watching news broadcasts and listening to my teachers and friends, and I have noticed the growing concern about MCAS testing. I think that more statewide after-school programs that focus on helping students prepare for the MCAS would eliminate this worry. These programs could probably result in a boost in enthusiasm for the test and higher overall scores.

Students would have another place to go after school. After-school programs could help stop the dangerous accidents that occur when children are left home alone. These programs could eliminate school-age students from being in shooting accidents or being caught in house fires. Also, instead of being busy with kids causing problems on the street after school, policemen can focus on other crimes.

Some people may argue that starting statewide after-school programs would be too expensive. But I think that over time, funds could be collected for the creation of these programs if it couldn't be done right away. Furthermore, the rewards of the programs would outweigh the costs.

I myself am a student that attends after school programs in the city of Boston. I believe that the program I attend, Citizen Schools, has helped me to become a better writer and public speaker. This program has also exposed me to resources I never even knew existed. Programs like this should be available beyond Boston and throughout the state.

Sincerely,

Naomi E. Brown

CHAPTER 9

Assignment 6
Book Review

A book review should not be confused with a book report: the former affects the lives of not only authors and book sellers but all manner of readers and thinkers (that is, almost everyone) and the latter is an assignment given in English class to prove that a student has read a book. A book report can easily be faked or copied; a book review, because of its persuasive nature, cannot. A book report is merely a list of facts; a book review requires the higher-level skills of evaluation and synthesis. Book reviews inform people not only about what titles are topical, but also what ideas are topical.

When students realize that book reviews can be found in newspapers, magazines and journals all around them, they begin to understand the magnitude of the genre. As an introduction for the class, I circulate recent book reviews from the local paper or popular magazines like *Sports Illustrated*. If possible, I try to find reviews about young adult literature or books in the news. Any book by Stephen King always kindles interest. A wonderful journal for middle school teachers called *Voices from the Middle* publishes reviews by middle school students in each issue. I especially like to use these as examples because of their brevity, book selections, and consistently strong introductions.

For this assignment I allow students to review any novel or memoir they've read recently, whether from English class, summer reading, independent school-time reading, or at-home personal reading. They must, however, consult the book while writing. I can provide copies of books in our curriculum, but beyond that, students must either bring their books from home or check them out of the library. Memory alone will not suffice; besides, I strongly recommend that students include excerpts. When the assignment is completed, I encourage students to submit their reviews to *Voices from the Middle* or to enter them at amazon.com.

Suggested Mini-Lessons

❏ 1 ELEMENTS OF A BOOK REVIEW

❏ 2 HOW TO HAVE AN OPINION ABOUT LITERATURE

❏ 3 HOMOPHONES

Materials: Copies of pages 51–55 for students.

Mini-Lesson 1
Elements of a Book Review

By examining some clippings of reviews from newspapers, magazines, and *Voices from the Middle*, students can draw some preliminary conclusions about what an effective book review should do. First, students notice that the review gives some information about the book, like characters, setting, plot, conflict, theme, page length, author, and writing style. I list these on the board. Often, a review provides a short excerpt from the book or a quotation, so the reader can experience for himself a bit of the writing style or plot. In addition, the reviewer gives an opinion about the book. The opinion can be strongly appreciative, strongly unfavorable, or anywhere in between. We discuss these elements, and students copy a summary in their notebooks.

For this assignment, I don't require students to list the page length, publisher, date of publication, or

Mini-Lesson 2
How to Have an Opinion About Literature

Rarely are students trained in this skill. I myself did not teach it until I realized that most students didn't know that a person was allowed to have in-depth opinions about literature. Areas like characters, plot and theme development, and writing style were sacred territory that they, the lowly students, were not in a position to judge. Most students, when asked for an evaluation of a book, went no further than: "It's good," "It's boring," "It's too long," or "I liked it." They understood what they were to do, but they didn't understand how they were to go about it or what questions they should ask themselves. Learning these skills early will prove invaluable for the high school and college years.

Students usually spend the first day choosing a book and assembling the facts about that book on the prewriting sheets. For this mini-lesson, I have students flip to the second prewriting sheet where there is space to record some opinions about their books. Most students at this point will have a basic positive or negative reaction: "I liked it" or "I didn't like it." I tell them to start with that, and then ask themselves why they did or did not like it, jotting down any thoughts that come to mind. From there, I guide them through some specific questions. As they write, I encourage them to elaborate, to be specific, and to cite parts of the story that pertain to their answers. (Sticky notes are quite handy for marking passages that could be of future use. I pass out a couple of pads and tell each student to take two or three sheets to start.) At the end of the lesson, I hand out a photocopy of the questions on page 54, which students can staple into their notebooks.

I direct students to refer to these questions again as they assemble their reviews. They need not address all ten questions in their reviews; they should employ the few that most resonate with them. All students should, however, include the answer to number 10 in their essays. If needed, it is a classic way to end a book review,

ISBN; providing the author and title is adequate.

I have students flip to the Ways to Start an Essay page in their notebooks, and we discuss how to adapt those techniques to this assignment. For example, the student could lift a sensory detail or scene right from the book; she could quote a character or a line of description. However the student chooses to begin the essay, I emphasize that she must segue immediately into giving the author's name, the book's title, and a taste of what her opinion will be; this information should be included in the first paragraph.

I give students the prewriting sheets (pages 52 and 53) to help them sort their thoughts. This assignment requires students to handle more information than in previous assignments, and brainstorming and grouping from scratch may prove too difficult. The prewriting sheet provides a space for brainstorming and suggests additional areas to examine. When the sheet is complete, students can organize the information into groups of their own choosing. You may find that some students need help remembering the meanings of terms such as *theme* or *conflict*. Usually these memory lapses can be reversed during individual conferences; if the whole class is at a loss, you may want to take a few minutes of class time to give a crash course.

though not the most original. I encourage students to experiment with other conclusions before using this acceptable but predictable standby.

Mini-Lesson 3
Homophones

We take a break from the intense series of language-enhancing techniques spread over the last few assignments to focus on a spelling skill. Homophones can pose unique spelling problems for writers because most word processing programs do not detect them as misspelled words. In addition, our language teems with them. In this short paragraph alone, there are more than a dozen homophones.

A question about homophones appears on the second E/R Check Sheet, so all students at this point are aware of them. Many students have been working on homophones since the first assignment, in conferences with me and on their Spelling Correction Sheets. I like to bring the topic up with the entire class, however, as the state tests draw near.

There are no shortcuts to proper homophone usage. Yes, some mnemonic techniques exist for certain homophones, but in general, the student must consult a

---

FREQUENTLY MISUSED HOMOPHONES

their, there, they're	dear, deer
capital, capitol	patience, patients
which, witch	bear, bare
principal, principle	site, cite, sight
to, too, two	four, for
die, dye	so, sew, sow
here, hear	break, brake
forth, fourth	stare, stair
herd, heard	I'll, aisle, isle
horse, hoarse	know, no
one, won	buy, by, bye
course, coarse	are, our

---

dictionary when in doubt. I draw attention to a home-made poster listing commonly confused homophones (see above) and introduce a fun reference book to students called *A Dictionary of Homophones* by Leslie Presson (Barrons Educational, 1997). I hope that the unintimidating slimness of the volume, along with the humorous cartoons, will motivate students to actually look up an unknown homophone, instead of guessing.

Homophones made up of contractions are especially misused, and these mistakes are glaring to state test graders. I hang a separate poster just for contraction and possessive homophones which looks like this:

CONTRACTIONS	POSSESSIVES
it's = it is	The dog wagged its tail.
who's = who is	Whose coat is this?
they're = they are	Their house sits on the corner.
you're = you are	Your book is new.

During the mini-lesson, I remind the class that an apostrophe takes the place of a missing letter; on the board, I diagram two words contracting into one, with an arrow mapping the dropped letter's metamorphosis into an apostrophe. (This diagram is often redrawn during individual conferences.)

If a student misspells a homophone on his final draft, I have him write not only the correct spelling but also its meaning on his Spelling Correction Sheet. If the homophone is a contraction or possessive, the student must write out the base words (as above) or the word "possessive" after the correct spelling. As explained in the first chapter, writing out correct spellings five times each serves as a strong motivator for most students. For students with learning disabilities that significantly hinder spelling ability, or even for second-language learners who struggle with homophones, I give extra practice after school with games like Homophone Rummy or Homophone Go Fish.

Name _____ Date _____ Period _____

 Assignment 6
Book Review

❏ Read the two sample book reviews and answer the following questions for each review.

   1. How does the review start?

   2. How does the review end?

   3. Find an example of the author's opinion and write it down.

❏ Think of a novel or memoir that you want to review. It doesn't have to be a book you liked, just one you know and understand well. If it is not a school book, you must find a copy yourself.

❏ Complete the prewriting sheet for this assignment.

❏ On another piece of paper, group your ideas into paragraphs.

❏ Write a rough draft of your review. It should be at least one typed page.

❏ Revise the draft. Check for:

_____ an interesting title

_____ an attention-grabbing introduction

_____ author's name and title of book

_____ at least one quote (punctuated correctly)

_____ transition words

_____ your opinion throughout

_____ a strong conclusion

❏ Reread your draft, and upgrade five verbs to stronger ones. Make sure your sentences are varied.

❏ Complete an E/R Check Sheet and revise again. Hand in your questions, prewriting sheet, groups sheet, rough draft(s), final copy, E/R Check Sheet, and this sheet.

		Preliminary Grade	Revised Grade
STRUCTURE (organization, paragraphs, length, font)	20 pts.	_____	_____
PROCESS (questions, prewrite, groups, rough draft, E/R Check Sheet)	20 pts	_____	_____
DESCRIPTION (title, intro, conclusion, quote, banned words, opinion, verbs, transition words, sentence variation)	20 pts.	_____	_____
SPELLING	20 pts.	_____	_____
GRAMMAR (punctuation, capitals, sentences, quotation marks, underlining book title, _____)	20 pts.	_____	_____
	TOTAL		_____

Name _____ Date _____ Period _____

Assignment 6

Book Review Prewriting Sheet 1

Title of book _____

Author _____

Brainstorm any ideas you have that might be useful in a review of this book:

_____

_____

_____

_____

_____

Give a BRIEF Summary:

_____

_____

_____

_____

List the main character(s):　　1. _____

　　　　　　　　　　　　　　2. _____

　　　　　　　　　　　　　　3. _____

What was the biggest struggle for the main character?

_____

_____

How was this struggle finally resolved?

_____

How did this character change during the story?

_____

_____

Book Review Prewriting Sheet 2

Looking at your answer to the previous question, what is the theme or message of this story?

_____

_____

How would you describe the author's writing style? (Think about vocabulary, sentence length, descriptions, the tone of voice of the narrator, and the overall mood of the book.)

_____

_____

Give one or two quotations from the book that support any of your answers above:

_____

_____

_____

_____

What is your opinion of the work? Use this space to jot down ideas concerning your feelings about this book. Use the questions from How to Have an Opinion About Literature.

_____

_____

_____

_____

_____

_____

_____

_____

On a separate sheet of paper, group your ideas into paragraphs. Weave your opinions in wherever they seem appropriate. Use quotations from the book to support your points.

BOOK REVIEW

How to Have an Opinion About Literature

1. Could you identify with the main character? Did he or she seem like a real person? Was he or she likeable? Could you picture him or her clearly? Was there enough description?

2. Did the other characters seem believable?

3. Did the place seem like a believable place? Did you feel as if you were there? Was there enough description of it?

4. Was the story itself interesting? Did it seem too slow or too fast? Did you believe that the events could have happened? Even the most outlandish sci-fi tale should somehow convince the reader of its credibility. For example, when you were reading the story, did you go along with it, as if it could be true, or did you say to yourself, "This could never happen. It's dumb."

5. Was the climax/resolution satisfying, or was it a letdown?

6. Do you feel that the main character learned something important? Did he or she change by the end of the story?

7. Did you enjoy the author's writing style? Why or why not?

8. What was a favorite part of the book? Why?

9. What was a part that you didn't like? Why?

10. Would you recommend this book to another reader? To a specific audience? Why?

BOOK REVIEW SAMPLES

Take *Out of the Dust* out of the Shelf

by Nadia Tubaishat, eighth grader

The dust hits the windows sharply, flying through the cracks into the house. "Brown earth rain[s] from the sky," pulling out plants and crops as it comes closer. The air chokes you and stings your eyes, making it hard for you to see and breathe. Would you like to live in these conditions? In *Out of the Dust* by Karen Hesse, the main character, Billie Jo, must face these problems, leading to an exciting read.

The novel is set in the Dust Bowl of Oklahoma in the 1920's. Billie Jo lives in a poor farming household with her father and expectant mother. The new baby is a joy to Billie Jo's father, since he hopes it is the boy he always wanted. Billie Jo has learned to get through the horrific dust storms with her love of music. Like her mother, she is a wonderful and talented piano player. However, in a tragic accident, Billie Jo's life is turned around. The house is set on fire by a burning pail of kerosene when "a rope of fire rose up from the stove to the pail." The results change the family forever.

After this incident, Billie Jo must cope with a lot. In the fire, Billie Jo lost the use of her hands, making her unable to play the piano. The piano was her only means of escape from her troubles, and now she couldn't play it. Billie Jo must cope with their increasing poverty and the horrific dust storms, along with the strained relationship between her and her father, whom she blames for everything.

One theme in *Out of the Dust* is that life goes on. It is a story about survival. Billie Jo must learn to forgive, face her problems, and continue living life. The book's free verse poetry structure and descriptive images make it an easy and enjoyable read as we accompany Billie Jo in her journey to find meaning amid suffering.

The Power of Imagination

by Ashley Hogan, eighth grader

Have you ever had an imaginary friend—or enemy—that was so strong it seemed real? *The Girl Who Loved Tom Gordon* by Stephen King is about a nine-year-old girl named Trisha MacFarland who got lost in the wilderness of Maine. She used her love for Tom Gordon, a closing pitcher for the Red Sox, to keep her company on her long and dangerous trek towards home. "By Saturday morning Tom Gordon had become her full-time companion, not pretend but accepted as real."

Trisha had been on a six-mile hike with her mother and older brother. Tired of the bickering between her mother and brother, she'd walked off to go to the bathroom and could not find her way back after that. Her family did not notice her absence, since they were fighting.

Trisha knew a little bit about being in the woods from her dad, but hadn't had any real-life experience. She had to struggle to try to get out of the woods and back to her family. In addition, she started to imagine a "thing" in the woods that was leaving a trail of slaughtered animals in her path. She was scared and weak, fighting for survival.

During her ordeal, Trisha gained a higher understanding of the wilderness. She learned what she could eat and what she should not drink. She invented strategies to keep her company while she searched and waited for help. Most importantly, Trisha learned that she must control her imagination and keep her head straight.

This novel is excellently written by an extraordinary author. It is at some points sad and at other points terrifying. I felt like I was a part of Trisha's wild adventure, following her path through the woods. I would highly recommend this book to anyone who loves adventure, suspense, and the outdoors.

CHAPTER 10

Assignment 7
Arts Review

If the Book Review was dinner, then the Arts Review is dessert. Students are at first surprised that they can write about topics like their favorite CDs or recently seen movies; they soon settle in to the task with focus and a sense of purpose. Even though they chose their books for the previous assignment, students tend to view the Book Review as teacher territory; now, they become the experts: surely they know more than I do about popular music and movies! In fact, I learn a lot from this assignment. Confidence, excitement, and motivation flourish.

Like book reviews, reviews of the arts proliferate our culture and affect the lives of artists, their respective industries, and consumers. It is easy to find reviews of music, movies, and theater in any local paper or magazine—I show the classes examples that I think will interest them. Sometimes I use one of these professional examples as an official sample essay for the assignment; nevertheless, I have included two student samples in this chapter.

Suggested Mini-lessons

☐ 1 EXPLANATION OF REVIEW; TOPICS

☐ 2 TONE

☐ 3 COMMAS AND FRAGMENTS

Materials: Copies of pages 59–62 for students.

Mini-Lesson 1
Explanation of Review; Topics

After looking at a few current professional examples, most students quickly understand what they are supposed to do. I make sure that I have at least one sample review of each "arts" genre allowed for this assignment: CDs, movies, plays, and concerts. As we read through each of the samples, I ask what elements make up the review, and we generate lists on the board which students copy into their notebooks. I then hand out How to Have an Opinion about the Arts (page 60), to be secured into their notebooks. During this mini-lesson, I read through the handout with students, but I don't have them take notes. Since they have already thought

through similar issues for the Book Review, I feel confident that they can do so again here without any hand-holding from me. As always, I can help whoever needs it during individual conferencing.

I emphasize that, as with the Book Review, this review need not be a completely favorable one: students are allowed to be lukewarm or even negative. As with all pieces of persuasion, supporting evidence is the key. Students must give examples and with CD reviews, a quotation. Quotes from movies are also encouraged; I tell students to remember what they can.

As always, I remind students to consult their notes on introductions and conclusions. Hopefully these methods are starting to sink in!

Students are now ready to write; hand out copies of the assignment and prewriting sheets if students have not gotten them already.

Mini-Lesson 2
Tone

At this point, I will have been coaching some students in tone for a few assignments, trying to help them temper a sarcastic voice or strengthen an insecure one. But for most students, the term is relatively new even though its meaning is not: they all know what it means when an adult says, "Tone it down" or "Don't take that tone with me." I give another example: one friend asks another how the day went and the second friend says, "Wonderful." In what different tones could this be said to communicate different meanings? Students try saying the word aloud and realize that different tones could communicate *opposite* meanings. Thus my point: tone carries meaning.

But how, they ask, can tone be conveyed in writing when there is no spoken voice? The best way to illustrate the answer is by having students peruse two short examples like these:

The incessant bass and screechy vocals make this album a punishment for your ears. If you like headaches and cacophony, then rush to the store to buy this CD.

The steady beat persists throughout the album and balances well with the singer's high, angelic voice. The blend is like heaven meeting Earth. If you enjoy music that differs from boring mainstream sound, then this CD is for you.

I ask students to imagine that these are about the same album. We discuss the writers' differing attitudes, and then create a list on the board regarding tone:

We can then compile a definition of tone which I shape into something close to this:

 Tone: The writer's attitude toward the subject, developed by word choice as well as images, description, and figurative language.

I emphasize that writers actively choose the tone they want, and I suggest that students be aware of their tone as they write. They should ask themselves, "Is the tone in this piece how I want it to sound? Is it too sarcastic or angry? Is it humorous when I want to be serious, or vice versa? What can I change to make it sound more like what I want?" It will take some time—years probably—for students to fully understand and master tone. But as with most of our topics this year, I am satisfied even if students only develop a mindfulness that these concepts exist. Students and I will revisit tone in our final preparation for the standardized tests, and I hope that this small seed of awareness might save a few points that would have otherwise been lost.

HOW WRITERS CREATE TONE

1. <u>By choice of words:</u>

   "headaches" and "cacophony"

   "boring mainstream"

2. <u>By choice of images and descriptions:</u>

   "incessant bass" and "screechy vocals" versus "steady beat" and "angelic voice"

3. <u>By choice of similes and metaphors:</u>

   "a punishment for your ears"

   "like heaven meeting Earth"

Mini-Lesson 3
Commas and Fragments

Anyone who teaches middle school knows that helping students understand fragments and run-ons can only be accomplished over a long (and sometimes frustrating) period of time—often years. In spite of this, we must continue to explain the conventions regarding these skills and have faith that someday, somewhere, it will all click in students' brains. I start at the beginning of the year in individual conferences helping students progress along the path to sentence fulfillment. This mini-lesson is for many a recap and for some a reminder, but it is not new information for anyone.

We start with the elements of a sentence. Many students understand that a sentence must have a subject and a verb; to that I add the all-important criterion that a sentence must be a complete thought. Certain single words can negate a complete thought, and I list these on a poster titled "Words that Need a Two-Part Sentence," since the inclusion of these words in a sentence, especially at the beginning, usually mandates a second, independent clause.

WORDS THAT NEED A TWO-PART SENTENCE

When	While
Even though	Although
Before	If

I realize that many exceptions exist to my rudimentary rule; my goal at this point is only to correct the most egregious sentence errors. I'm teaching sentence survival here. For more advanced writers, I can explain the finer points of dependent and independent clauses, or even colon and semicolon use, during individual conferences. I illustrate my "Two-Part" rule by singling out a student and saying in an expectant voice, "When school is over

this afternoon," and then turning from her. To another student I say, inflecting my voice and raising my eyebrows, "If I have enough money" and then stop abruptly. Students quickly get it. One must finish the thought. Most two-part sentences, I remind them, need a comma between the clauses.

The second major obstacle to sentence proficiency is when students use a comma in place of a period, thereby creating a run-on. I tell them that if they are unsure about a comma in their paper, they should ask themselves two basic questions:

1. Is this a two-part sentence?

2. Is this comma accompanied by a conjunction?

(For a quick review of conjunctions, I teach students a simple acronym: FANBOYS. It stands for *for, and, nor, but, or, yet,* and *so.* I remind students that "for" as a conjunction is an old-fashioned way of saying "because," and "yet" as a conjunction means "but.")

If either of these answers is no, the student should ask himself if the comma should be a period. Again, I realize this is an oversimplification of comma usage, but my goal is to focus on where mistakes are made. Most students know that certain commas are always correct, such as ones used in lists or with appositives. It is the comma that pastes together a run-on that I want to eradicate. By giving students just a few simple rules, the majority of mistakes can be prevented. Of course, the key to solidifying students' understanding of these conventions lies in using their own work for examples. In individual conferences, I can repeat and apply these rules, tailoring my instruction. For some students, I may even review a photocopied drill of ten fragments or run-ons with them for extra practice. In every case, though, I let go of my need to perfect when the student reaches frustration level.

Assignment 7

Arts Review

❏ Read the two sample reviews. Answer the following questions for each review:

    1. How does the review begin?

    2. How does the review end?

    3. Describe the writer's tone, and find examples to support your ideas.

❏ You will write a review of a CD, movie, play, or concert. Choose one of these to write about.

❏ Complete both sides of the prewriting sheet.

❏ On another sheet of paper, group your ideas into paragraphs.

❏ Write a rough draft, enough for at least one typed page.

❏ You MUST begin and end in interesting ways. Check your notebook for ideas.

❏ Think of a clever title. Don't just use the title of the movie, CD, or play.

❏ Make sure you've used some transition words, and then upgrade some of your verbs. Don't start two sentences the same way in the same paragraph.

❏ Complete an E/R Check Sheet and revise again.

❏ Hand in the final copy with your prewriting sheet, groups, rough drafts, E/R Check Sheet, and this sheet.

		Preliminary Grade	Revised Grade
STRUCTURE (organization, paragraphs, length, font)	20 pts.	_____	_____
PROCESS (questions, prewrite, groups, rough, E/R Check Sheet)	20 pts.	_____	_____
DESCRIPTION (title, quotes, intro, conclusion, opinion, banned words, verbs, transition words, sentence variation)	20 pts.	_____	_____
SPELLING	20 pts.	_____	_____
GRAMMAR (punctuation, capitals, sentences, quotation marks, _____)	20 pts.	_____	_____
	TOTAL		_____

ARTS REVIEW

How to Have an Opinion About the Arts

CDs

1. Is the style of music enjoyable? Why or why not?

2. Is the style of music original? If so, explain exactly in what way. If not, whom does it imitate?

3. Are the lyrics interesting or original? Why or why not? Quote some examples.

4. What other words would you use to describe the lyrics? Tell why.

5. Are all the songs on the CD well done, or are there only one or two hits? Explain.

6. Are all the songs similar, or do they cover a range of topics, emotions, and musical styles? Give examples. How do you feel about this?

7. How does this CD compare with the artist's/artists' previous CDs? How do you feel about this?

8. Overall, would you recommend this CD to other consumers? Would you recommend it to a specific audience? Why or why not?

MOVIES

1. Could you identify in some way with the main character(s)? Did they seem believable? Could real people behave like that? If not, explain why.

2. Did the scenery add to the story? How? How else would you describe the scenery?

3. Was the story too slow or too fast? Did it seem like the events could have really happened?

4. Was the ending satisfying? Did the characters change? Did you like the ending? Explain.

5. Were the actors believable, or did they seem like they were "just acting" at some points? When?

6. Did the actors work well together—did brothers seem like brothers, spouses like spouses, best friends like best friends? At any time did you think, *She's not really feeling that. She's just acting.* When?

7. Overall, would you recommend this movie to other people? To a specific audience? Explain.

PLAYS

1. Read through the questions for Movies and answer them. Keep in mind that theater is much more restricted with scenery than movies.

2. Was the scenery creative? Did it help you understand the play? Was it elaborate or sparse? Give examples. How did you feel about this?

3. Did there seem to be an energy between the actors and the audience? Explain. How did you feel about this?

4. Were any of the actors too quiet or difficult to understand? Were there any forgotten lines? Were any of the actors clearly outstanding?

5. Would you recommend this play? Explain.

CONCERTS

1. Was the sound of the singers and instruments enjoyable? Explain.

2. Did the scenery add to the music, or detract? Explain.

3. Was there an energy or excitement in the air? Describe. How did you feel?

4. Did the lead singer connect with the crowd? How?

5. Were there any extras, such as dancing, stories, fireworks, or people flying through the air? Were there any surprises? How did you feel about any of these, or their absence?

6. Would you recommend that other people see this concert? Why or why not?

Name _____ Date _____ Period _____

Assignment 7

Arts Review Prewriting Sheet

Name of Work _____

Artist (for CDs) or Performer(s) (for plays, movies, or concerts):

_____

_____

_____

Brainstorm any ideas about the work:

_____

_____

_____

_____

_____

_____

_____

Facts about the Work:

List some factual information about the work. For example, give the genre, characters, setting, plot, and theme for movies and plays; give the style, length, and themes of CDs and concerts.

_____

_____

_____

_____

Read How to Have an Opinion About the Arts and note your answers below. Use the back of this sheet if you need more space.

_____

_____

_____

_____

_____

_____

Look over all you have written on this sheet. On a separate sheet, group your ideas into paragraphs. Remember, you need not use every idea you have written, and you can add other ideas, too.

"You Can Run, You Can Hide, But You Can't Escape" Enrique

by Ashlee Sweeney, eighth grader

Does the name Enrique Iglesias sound familiar? If not, it will soon. He is the new Latin sensation, and the son of famous vocalist Julio Iglesias. He exploded onto the pop music scene with his second English language album, "Escape" released in November, 2001.

This first hit on Enrique's CD is the love ballad "Hero." This song has a different meaning for different people in America. Since the single was released around September, 2001, some people refer to it as the song of the 9/11 heroes. I feel that the lyrics are too sappy and romantic to be about people risking their lives. However, it is a superb choice for a wedding song, or a song to declare one's love to another. On "Escape" there are two versions of the song: one in English, and the other in Spanish, Iglesias' native language.

What I love about this CD is how much emotion Enrique puts into every song. He is not a male Britney Spears, who uses a synthesizer while talking about love. He uses his real voice and his real soul to get the audience into the song. The style is so pure, yet so simple. No other vocal artist has mastered putting so much pure emotion in a song. A line from the above-mentioned hit "Hero" is, "I will stand by you forever / You can take my breath away." While singing that, the once bashful Enrique crescendos on the "forever," adding a strong impact to the words' meaning. On the next line he becomes softer on "breath away." It is a purposeful art that makes the song beautiful.

Enrique doesn't just sing ballads. His songs can all be related to love, but not all of them have slow beats. One song, "Don't Turn Off the Lights," has a bouncy, catchy beat that is not overdone. Another bonus to this CD is that there are no expletives. Some of the deeper meanings of the songs contain some mature material, but it isn't obvious to a younger audience.

"Escape" is one of those CDs you won't get bored of hearing. The mixture of ballads and dance songs create a more mature sound for Enrique than on his first album. You will be dancing with the beat, and sighing with the ballads.

"The Ring" Rings in Totals at Box Office

by Nadia Tubaishat, eighth grader

Rachel is pushed into the abandoned well. She falls further and further, on her last day to live. She reaches the bottom and lies unconscious in the water. An image comes to her mind and she suddenly realizes what happened to Semara. This could save her and her son's life.

The movie "The Ring" is like the next "Sixth Sense." This horror tale with its gruesome effects and twists is another story of the dead communicating with the living, but to a different extent. Rachel's (Naomi Watts) niece, Katie, watches a tape while out vacationing with her friends. Seven days later, Katie and her friends all die. Rachel, a reporter, decided to look into the case, since there was an urban myth circulating that whoever viewed the tape would die. The tape ends up in Rachel's hands. After watching it, she gets a phone call telling her she has "seven days to live." Her ex-husband, Noah, and young son, Aidan also watched the tape, and together Rachel and Noah work to figure out how to stop their deaths. The tape itself is disturbing but includes the symbols that could lead Rachel to the answers.

The special effects and gruesome images throughout the movie add tension to the story. However, the best feature of the movie is its plot twists that turn the story around at the end creating an unexpected conclusion. Just when the movie seems to end, it is only the beginning of the climax. The ending is also very satisfying.

Although this movie only received moderate reviews, I thought it was excellent. The public must have also agreed because it was the highest grossing film of November, 2002. It is meant to scare and it succeeds, keeping the viewer in suspense for days *after* watching the film. It would not be a waste of money to see this movie; I assure you, you will be scared.

CHAPTER 11

Assignment 8
Personal Essay

This assignment is nothing new; in fact, it dates back to the sixteenth century, when Michel de Montaigne retired from public life and wrote essays that combined his own musings with quotations he had come across in his reading. Most students, however, have never heard of such a genre, and often need a little encouragement getting started. I came up with the idea for this assignment during a graduate literature course, while reading Francis Bacon, who wrote 50 years after Montaigne. Bacon walked around with a notebook full of interesting quotations that he regularly added to. The quotations were arranged by topic, and he would jot down his own ideas about the topics as well. Eventually, drawing from his notebook, he wrote his famous *Essays*, meditations on such subjects as love, friendship, and books. (I later discovered that some of Montaigne's essays were titled "On war-horses," "On the custom of wearing clothing," "On the Cannibals," and "That we should not be deemed happy till after our death.") While sitting in the class, I thought, "Eighth graders could do this." They certainly have enough opinions; why not get them to organize and focus them, and do a bit of research as well?

For the assignment, I round up some quotation dictionaries from various libraries (including my own) and give students a detailed prewriting guide (page 66). In the guide, I ask them to choose a topic and then write their opinion on the topic; this essay is, in the end, a persuasive essay. They must then come up with an example from their own lives that illustrates their beliefs or in some way illuminates the topic. I also ask students to think of art such as movies, books, poems, or songs that deal with the topic. This is usually easier than the autobiographical part, since most teens remember movies in more detail than they do their own lives. In addition, when writing about movies and books they risk no embarrassment in revelation.

Next, students consult the quotation dictionaries and find a quote that they understand and that is relevant to their opinion. This requires real concentration on their part. Of course, I explain the quotations to any student who asks for help. I want them to understand that they have to be in charge of the research they use; they can't simply copy down the first quotation they find.

By now we've been working on introductions for some time. I tell students to use their own judgment: maybe they want to use the autobiography snippet, maybe the quotation, maybe the dictionary definition. I realize that for experienced writers, the dictionary definition is an easy way in. But I like to let beginners experiment with anything that seems interesting to them.

This assignment utilizes skills in description, persuasion, autobiography, and research. The Personal Essay is an excellent introduction to the research papers that students will do in high school, if they have not written some already. In looking for quotations, students must understand and analyze other people's words. How often have we as teachers read research papers in which the student obviously did not understand the research she was citing? In addition, quotations from a

Suggested Mini-Lessons

❏ 1 PERSONAL ESSAY DEFINED; HOW TO USE A QUOTATION DICTIONARY

❏ 2 QUOTING WITHIN THE ESSAY

❏ 3 WORDS INSTEAD OF "SAID"

Materials: *Copies of pages 65–68 for students.*

quotation dictionary are usually short, therefore providing a nonthreatening introduction to the art of research. Finally, using quotation marks and giving the author's name prepares them for the more extensive citation logistics of a formal research paper.

What I like best about this assignment, though, is reading the papers that come in. Students enjoy shaping and crafting their opinions, and the topics are ones that they might not otherwise have a chance to reflect on in writing, unless it's in connection with something else—a novel or poem, for example. In writing this essay, students must rely on their own thoughts and experiences without any springboards. The thoughts of others are used only as a backup to their own. Each year, this assignment gives me new insights into students, and I believe they get new insights into themselves: many students are not natural philosophers, and even if they are, they rarely are asked to think all the way through a topic and develop a cohesive argument. And even the kids who grumble at the introduction of this assignment eventually find a topic that interests them. Once that happens, the ideas start flowing and even my toughest critics hand in their papers with a look of satisfaction. This assignment proves what I will always believe: kids, and all of us, enjoy thinking. It just feels good.

Mini-Lesson 1
Personal Essay Defined; How to Use a Quotation Dictionary

I ask students if they've ever heard of such a genre, or if not, what they think it might be. Usually, once we start discussing it, one student will say, "Oh, it's like a *Chicken Soup for the Soul* assignment." I introduce Montaigne and Bacon to them. We discuss possible topics; I stress that if an abstract topic like "friendship" or "trust" seems too difficult, they can choose something concrete like "school" or "soccer."

I explain to students that one part of the essay will involve using other people's ideas to support their own, and that one way to do this is to use a quotation dictionary. After soliciting topics from students, I demonstrate how to use the books, and read a few quotes. Then I pass around the books so they can see for themselves. Students enjoy discovering entertaining quotations (who doesn't?), so I have to make sure they don't get too absorbed in the books.

Mini-Lesson 2
Quoting Within the Essay

I go over how to use quotation marks, and stress that students must give the author's name either somewhere in the sentence or in parentheses at the end of the sentence. This is a wonderful preparation for a future research paper, when students would include not only the quotation itself and the author's name, but the page number as well.

Mini-Lesson 3
Words Instead of "Said"

I've included this mini-lesson with this assignment not only because of the cited quotation, but also because students must write a bit of autobiography, which often contains speaking. I reiterate to the classes that effective writers search for interesting, precise words. For this lesson, I want them to focus their verb-enhancing skills on a single word: *said*. I reassure students that they already know plenty of interesting words; the trick is to dig them up, and to use the right word in the right place. I write "said" on the board, and ask the class to brainstorm for any other "speaking" words that they know. Once the first few alternatives are volunteered, the class starts firing words so quickly that I can hardly keep up. Students offer words like *taunted*, *warned*, *stammered*, *chortled*, *bellowed*, *croaked*, and *purred*. At the end of each class, I record the words and at the end of the day, I compile all the lists. I transfer the compilation onto a poster that we can use as a reference; it usually displays more than 80 words. I've included our list in Appendix C, though it is most effective to have classes generate their own lists.

Name _____ Date _____ Period _____

Assignment 8
Personal Essay

☐ Read the two sample essays. Write your answers to the following questions for each essay:

    1. What does the author use for an introduction?

    2. How does the author draw from personal experience?

    3. What is the opinion/main idea of the essay?

☐ Choose a topic for your own personal essay. Some examples are below, but you can choose anything that is appropriate for school. Look at your Topics for Writing for additional help.

☐ Some topics:

Truth	Envy	Gossip	Dating	Bravery
Fashion	Happiness	Sadness	Parents	Beauty
Youth	Nature	Writing	History	Lying
Sports	Solitude	Conscience	Loss	Popularity

☐ Fill out the prewriting sheet for this assignment.

☐ Group your ideas on a separate sheet of paper.

☐ Write a first draft and then type it. It should be at least one typed page.

☐ Revise the draft. Check for the following:

_____ a title: "On . . ."   _____ transition words

_____ an attention-grabbing introduction   _____ a quotation

_____ a true story   _____ strong verbs (change at least three)

_____ sentence variation   _____ a strong conclusion

☐ Complete an Editing/Revising Check Sheet and print out a final copy.

☐ Hand in the final copy with your prewriting sheet, groups, rough drafts, E/R Check Sheet, and this sheet.

		Preliminary Grade	Revised Grade
STRUCTURE (organization, paragraphs, length, font)	20 pts.	_____	_____
PROCESS (questions, prewrite, groups, rough, E/R Check Sheet)	20 pts.	_____	_____
DESCRIPTION (title, intro, conclusion, examples, banned words verbs, transition words, sentence variation)	20 pts.	_____	_____
SPELLING	20 pts.	_____	_____
GRAMMAR (punctuation, capitals, sentences, quotation marks, _____)	20 pts.	_____	_____
	TOTAL	_____	

Name _____ Date _____ Period _____

Assignment 8
Personal Essay Prewriting Sheet

What topic will your essay be about? _____

Write down a definition of your topic (either your own or from the dictionary):

_____
_____
_____

Write down your personal feelings or opinion about your topic. Is it beneficial? Useful? Harmful?
Important? Easy? Difficult? Common? Rare? What do you want to say about it? Brainstorm some ideas:

_____
_____
_____

Think of one or two real-life stories that illustrate your topic and your feelings about it. For example, if
you're writing about the dangers of anger, you could tell about a time when you (or someone) got angry
and lost a friendship or something else important. This should be a true story from your life.

_____
_____
_____

Look up a quote related to your topic. Copy that quote and its author. You can use more than one.

_____
_____
_____

Think about other examples that illustrate your topic (from books, short stories, poems, movies, etc.).
Add them:

_____
_____
_____

What's your final conclusion about your topic?

_____

What is an interesting way to start this essay? Write a first sentence below:

_____

On a sheet of loose-leaf paper, take these ideas and group them in an order that seems right to you.

PERSONAL ESSAY SAMPLES

On Truth

by Nadia Tubaishat, eighth grader

"Honesty; the real state of things" is how truth is defined in the Merriam-Webster Dictionary. But what is truth? Is it a positive or negative concept? Can it build friendships or break them? I think truth can have a two-dimensional aspect.

On one hand, truthfulness is a very strong quality. You need to be able to tell the truth and be honest to build relationships. It is healthier to get into the habit of telling the truth, even if there are consequences. If you lie all your life and the truth finally comes out, you will be faced with more consequences than before. If you are a truthful person, you will gain more respect from people and build more trusting relationships.

A couple of weeks ago, I went over my friend's house. We were planning to walk down to McDonald's and CVS from her house, which was a pretty far distance away. I debated telling my mom this, wondering if she would let me go. In the end, I decided to stay out of trouble and avoid the consequence of my mother finding me down there without permission. Even though she was concerned, she still let me go after I informed her. However, my other friend that was also over our friend's house didn't tell her mother. She got into trouble for lying, and was grounded for one week.

"The truth shall set you free" (Bible, John 8:32). I avoided losing my parent's trust by telling the truth; however, my friend didn't. Parents and children must tell the truth to build relationships. As kids grow older and are more independent, it is their responsibility to tell the truth to their parents about where they are going. Children who tell the truth to their parents are usually more respected by their parents and have more freedom and trust. However, children who do not tell the truth are usually more restricted and in more trouble.

Although truth is beneficial, there can be another view on it. "All truth is good, but not all truth is good to say" (Anonymous African Proverb). While being honest helps, it can also be dangerous. If you are brutally honest and mean to someone, they will be hurt and you may lose them as a friend. For example, if a friend gets a haircut that they like, and you tell them it is horrible, you will probably hurt your friend. If you are constantly revealing to people your negative opinions of them (all your true feelings), more people are going to find you rude and dislike you.

Truth can be helpful and hurtful either way. It is sometimes hard to know when to tell the truth. Truth can get you respected, or truth can get you hated. In the end, one must use his or her own judgment.

PERSONAL ESSAY SAMPLES

On History

by Annemarie Folan, eighth grader

History is our past, present, and future. It takes place every day even if we don't realize it. We see historic events every day in books, movies, television and all around us. "History has been conceived as the human struggle for civilization against barbarism in different ages and places, from the beginning of human societies" (Mary Ritter Beard).

I personally think that history is a very important part of life. Sometimes in history we made mistakes, so we know in the present not to make the same ones. If we didn't have history where would we be? We would be oblivious to anything from our pasts and futures without our history.

On the first day of school my Social Studies teacher declared, "We are tomorrow's history." A few days later, ironically, the incidents of September eleventh happened. It just goes to show that we are making our own history day by day.

When I think of history I usually think of war for some reason. I think we all get benefits from war even if it doesn't seem so. It is horrible, but when our country wins we get a sense of victory all around the country. Without war we would all still be under the control of England. Without some rebellion in our past we would not be Americans. We would all be British. If not for war in our history we might not have the fifty states like we do now. For example, we wouldn't have the state of Texas if the people there hadn't rebelled against the Mexicans.

History is always present in the media. Many movies focus on times in our past. Some examples are "The Patriot," "Pearl Harbor," "Amistad," and "Life Is Beautiful," among many more. Also, history is found in books that we read. I myself enjoy reading a series called the "Dear America" books which focus on important events in American history. I'm also in the middle of reading *The Diary of Anne Frank*. Even in English books for school, history is present. My favorite book that I've read in school, *The Devil's Arithmetic*, focuses on the Holocaust and one girl's understanding of it.

History is in all of us. Our mistakes and our actions change the world we live in and the world our descendants will live in. Without history we would be completely different than we are now, and we would not live in the world that we do today.

CHAPTER 12

Assignment 9
Short Story Analysis

The practice of analysis seems like a natural destination for the assignments in this book, since it combines elements of description, explanation, comparison, and persuasion. It is not likely that an analysis will be required of middle school students on a standardized test; descriptive or persuasive essays seem to be the norm. Many high school-level standardized tests, however, do require an analytical essay. I've included these final two assignments because the thinking and writing skills introduced here are the ones needed in mature academic settings such as high school, college, and beyond.

This assignment differs from the Book Review in that students must think more deeply about the material. Instead of gleaning a few main ideas from an entire novel, students will look closely at a single short story. Instead of stating the facts, such as "Huckleberry Finn is the main character of the book," students must ask themselves, "What *about* Huck Finn?" The answer should be debatable, as in, "Huck Finn learned more by running away than he would have learned in school." In the Book Review, I introduced the general notion of criticizing literature; now, I want students to realize that in an analysis, *most* of the ideas about the story should be arguments. It will require more thinking; it will require them to rely on their own thoughts. For many students, the transition from reporting the facts to interpreting the facts is a difficult one to make. At the same time, previous assignments should have prepared them for this moment. Their attempts will not be perfect; at this point, I try only to introduce, to open a door. Future teachers in high school and college can delve further into the training of thesis formulation and the interpretation of literature.

> ## Suggested Mini-Lessons
>
> ☐ 1 INTRODUCTION TO ANALYSIS; PARTS OF A SHORT STORY
>
> ☐ 2 AVOIDING "YOU"
>
> ☐ 3 KEEPING THE SAME TENSE THROUGHOUT
>
> **Materials:** Copies of pages 72–75 for students.

Mini-Lesson 1
Introduction to Analysis; Parts of a Short Story

Some students may already know the definition of *analysis*, or, more likely, *analyze*. I explain that they will choose a short story from this year's—or last year's—English class, and examine its parts in an attempt to get at the deeper meaning of the story. (Rarely are middle school students reading collections of short stories on their own. I gather extra copies of the school's texts for my classroom library.)

We review the main parts of a story, most of which they know and have used already in writing the Book Review. These include *characters*, *setting*, *plot*, and *theme*. To this I add *conflict*, and review the basic types of conflict (character vs. nature, character vs. character, character vs. society, character vs. self, and character vs. the supernatural). I emphasize that most compelling stories have at least two of these conflict categories

---

SOME WAYS TO ANALYZE LITERATURE

1. Look closely at the characters and make judgments about them.

   For example, don't just write, "The main character is a mongoose named Rikki Tikki Tavi." Ask yourself, "What about Rikki Tikki Tavi?" Instead try: "Rikki Tikki Tavi had to improve mentally and physically in order to kill Nag."

2. Look at the conflicts and explain them fully.

   Especially Character vs. Self: what do the characters wrestle with inside themselves?

3. Look closely at the theme and interpret it in your own words.

   Don't simply write, "The theme of this story is survival." Instead, ask yourself: What more can I explain about the author's view of survival? What does survival mean in this particular story?

4. Look for images in the book that might be symbols for something deeper.

   Instead of merely noticing "The setting has a lot of water in it," try to interpret what the water symbolizes: Fear? Mystery? Death? Abundance of life?

---

layered within the plot; students should search them out, and not simply be satisfied with the first conflict that comes to mind. I also note that when writing about short stories, students should put the story's title in quotation marks.

Most importantly, I explain to students that I want them to start thinking beyond the facts of the story; I want them to interpret. In the Book Review they looked at books from a consumer's point of view; now I want them to look with the eyes of a scholar-in-training. They should assume already that the story is "good" and proceed from there. In addition, they need not worry about revealing the ending, since an analysis requires full examination. I list on the board some helpful techniques.

This assignment requires original thinking from students; they must push themselves. I stress to students that the answers to these questions will be opinions, ideas that another person could debate. (I illustrate by refuting my examples above.) In a sense, there are no "right" answers. However, students must support their opinions with evidence from the story. Though it is hard to pinpoint one "correct" analysis of a story, certain interpretations can be more accurate than others. Interpretations that draw heavily from evidence in the story are the strongest.

Most students will struggle with this new challenge. In the individual conferences, once I see where a student is thinking, I can pose specific questions that will help him.

As stated earlier, my goal at this point is to simply introduce the idea of opinion and interpretation as the basis of literary criticism; in future months, and years, students will hone this skill.

Mini-Lesson 2
Avoiding "You"

I make public an idea that I've been circulating all year in individual conferences: don't use the pronoun *you*, meaning "a person in general," in writing. (Obviously the pronoun can be used within quotes, titles, a direct question to the reader in the introduction, and so on.) I want to eradicate the careless, generic "you" that pervades the language. For standardized test graders, who are mostly English teachers themselves, encountering an unspecified "you" is like hitting a pothole in the road. So I like to take a few minutes to address this bad habit with the entire class as the state tests approach.

If time allows, I may give a brief overview of first, second, and third persons; some students will already know these. Changing the second person "you" into the first person "I" or a third person noun like "one" will fix the problem. Rearranging the sentence so no reference at all is needed would also suffice. I caution that using "one" often leads to awkward pronoun requirements later in the sentence. We look at an example:

> When you read "The Tell Tale Heart" you feel like you are there.

I have students generate alternatives in their notebooks, and then write a few on the board:

> When one reads "The Tell Tale Heart" he/she feels like he/she is there.

(Students realize the clumsiness. I explain that they can choose one gender or alternate genders throughout the paper.)

> When I read "The Tell Tale Heart" I felt like I was there.

(First person, past tense)

> The reader of "The Tell Tale Heart" is immediately drawn in to the world of the narrator.

("You" changed to third person "reader"; ideas better worded)

As I have done all year, I circle any instances of "you" in students' papers and subtract points in the grammar category. During individual conferences, I can help strugglers find the words they need.

Mini-Lesson 3
Keeping the Same Tense Throughout

Unconsciously switching tenses is another grammatical main offender that I battle in individual conferences throughout the year, and as testing time nears, I like to present it in a mini-lesson almost as a review. We list the three major tenses and I state plainly that writers should not unknowingly switch among them. Besides being grammatically incorrect, it's downright confusing for the reader. Most frequently, students oscillate between present and past. I tell them to pick one and stick with it. When grading, I choose the tense that occupies most of the paper and underline all verbs in the other tense.

There are, of course, acceptable ways to switch tenses, but these should be obvious and intentional. For example, an essay written in present tense that includes an autobiographical anecdote in the past is not grammatically incorrect. Students understand this. It is the unmindful vacillation between tenses that I want them to stop.

Throughout the year, in individual conferences, the opportunity may arise to discuss other tenses, such as the perfect tenses. If used properly, these tenses do not interfere with the non-switch rule. I usually do not present these tenses to classes as a whole, however, unless time and academic level permit.

Assignment 9
Short Story Analysis

❏ Read the two sample essays. Write your answers to the following questions for each essay.

> **1.** What does the writer do for an introduction?
>
> **2.** What does the writer do for a conclusion?
>
> **3.** Find one statement in the essay that is a debatable interpretation.

❏ Choose a short story to analyze. Look through some of the books in the classroom to find one to write about. It should be a story that you've already read.

❏ Complete the prewriting sheet for this assignment.

❏ On another piece of paper, group your ideas into paragraphs.

❏ Write a rough draft, enough for at least one typed page.

❏ Create an interesting introduction and conclusion.

❏ Make sure you've used: _____ the story title and author's name

                                 _____ a quote from the story

                                 _____ some transition words

                                 _____ four new, stronger verbs

                                 _____ varied sentences

                                 _____ an interesting title

❏ Complete an E/R Check Sheet and revise again.

❏ Hand in the final copy with your brainstorming, prewriting, groups, rough drafts, E/R Check Sheet, and this sheet.

		Preliminary Grade	Revised Grade
STRUCTURE (organization, paragraphs, length, font)	20 pts.	_____	_____
PROCESS (questions, prewrite, groups, rough, E/R Check Sheet)	20 pts.	_____	_____
DESCRIPTION (title, intro, conclusion, examples, banned words verbs, transition words, sentence variation)	20 pts.	_____	_____
SPELLING	20 pts.	_____	_____
GRAMMAR (punctuation, capitals, sentences, tense, quotation marks, _____)	20 pts.	_____	_____
	TOTAL		_____

Short Story Analysis Prewriting Sheet 1

Title of story _____ **Author** _____

Brainstorm any ideas about this story that stand out in your mind.

_____

_____

_____

_____

_____

_____

_____

_____

Give a BRIEF summary of the story.

_____

_____

_____

_____

Analysis means looking at a story's parts. Take notes on some of the parts of this story.

1. The main character(s): _____

_____

_____

2. The setting:

_____

_____

_____

_____

3. What were some of the conflicts in the story? _____

_____

_____

_____

Short Story Analysis Prewriting Sheet 2

4. How does the main character change during the story? What does he or she learn?

_____

_____

_____

5. Based on what you wrote for number 4, what is the theme or message of this story?

_____

_____

_____

6. Give one or two quotes from the story that support any of your answers above.

_____

_____

_____

Look in your notebook at Some Ways to Analyze Literature. Read through the questions and note some answers below.

1. Characters: _____

_____

_____

2. Conflicts: _____

_____

3. Theme: _____

_____

4. Symbols: _____

_____

_____

Now, on a separate sheet of paper, organize your ideas into paragraph groups.

A Lesson Well Learned

by Eileen Molloy, eighth grader

When people are with others that are just like themselves, it is easier to get along with them. However, if a new, different type of person is introduced, he/she is treated as an unequal, and often left out. When this happens, people should look beyond differences, find similarities, and get along as best they can. This, I think, is the main message in Ray Bradbury's "All Summer in a Day."

In this story, the main character, Margot, is an Earth girl who moved to Venus when she was four. On Venus, it rains all the time except for an hour every seven years. Unlike her classmates, Margot can still remember the sun and how it shines. She desperately awaits the day when the sun will shine, but on that one day the children in her class lock Margot in a closet. After they play in the sun, they realize what Margot missed so much and they feel horrible.

The main conflict in this story is character vs. society because Margot wants to fit in and constantly has to fight off what her peers say about her. "Margot stood apart from them, from these children who could never remember a time when it didn't rain and rain and rain." This is a part of another conflict within the children themselves: the jealousy they had toward Margot for being able to remember the sun.

I think the sun is a symbol of peace. Once the children see the sun, they know what Margot missed, and they apologize to her.

Margot learns that though people can be cruel, they are not all evil at heart. The other kids learn that although someone may be different, he/she should still be accepted. I think they also learned that people shouldn't be jealous, because if they are, they cannot see the best qualities of a person past all the jealousy. "All Summer in a Day" illustrates a variety of human natures and tendencies.

Human Prey

by Ryan Kelly, eighth grader

Imagine being invited to go hunting only to discover that you are the prey. "The Most Dangerous Game" by Richard Connell is a story about life and the value of it. In this story, Sanger Rainsford is forced to flee for his life while General Zaroff hunts him down. Zaroff is an extreme hunter who has killed every animal and now hunts humans.

The story begins when Rainsford, a rich hunter on his way to a Hunting expedition in the Amazon, hears noises while his yacht approaches "Ship-Trap Island." A passenger on the yacht explains, "The old charts call it 'Ship-Trap Island.' A suggestive name, isn't it? Sailors have a curious dread of the place. I don't know why. Some superstition—" Rainsford later falls off his boat, trying to get a look at the island. On the island, Rainsford finds that Zaroff is kind at first, but he is mistaken: Zaroff wants to hunt him.

Rainsford amazed me with the skills he uses to survive a murderer. Rainsford has to use his own hunting skills to survive Zaroff's jungle. He climbs a tree without leaving a trace and builds a trap that kills one attack dog. Finally, he jumps off a cliff to save himself, and Zaroff thinks he is dead. At this point, I also thought the story was over. I thought it was a horrible ending, but when Rainsford reappears in Zaroff's bedroom that night and kills him, I was thrilled.

The main conflict that Rainsford has to deal with is character vs. character. He is chased around by a crazy man who loves to kill. In the end, he outsmarts him. However, another conflict that is just as strong is Rainsford vs. himself. Throughout the hunt, Rainsford tells himself to stay calm: "'I must keep my nerve. I must keep my nerve,' he said through tight teeth." His ability to keep his reason is what saves him.

A main theme of this story is determination, for both characters. Zaroff is determined to kill Rainsford, and Rainsford is determined to survive and escape. Another theme is the value of life. In the beginning of the story, Rainsford tells a shipmate, "'The world is made up of two classes—the hunters and the huntees. Luckily, you and I are hunters.'" I don't think he would say the same at the end of his ordeal as a "huntee" and even calls himself a "beast at bay" before he murders Zaroff. Richard Connell has skillfully illustrated the thin line between humans and animals in this action-packed story.

CHAPTER 13

Assignment 10
Analysis of a Poem

Although reviewing books and analyzing short stories, especially with the intensity presented in this book, may be somewhat new for students, looking closely at prose is not a foreign idea for most. Rarely, however, are students asked to write in-depth analyses of poems at the middle school level. If you have not been reading poems all year with your class, take a few days now to look at several poems, so that students can become familiar with concepts such as simile and metaphor, personification, alliteration, onomatopoeia, assonance, free verse, and stanza. Appendix C contains lists of poems (other than the poems in this chapter) that would help illustrate the above poetic techniques. To that basis of knowledge, we will now add aspects of form: rhyme scheme and meter. The mini-lessons for each of these run a bit long, but students catch on relatively quickly, and I help the confused ones in individual conferences. If you can, take as much time as students need to practice what the mini-lessons present, especially with the third mini-lesson, Linking Form and Content. Students' papers will be richer for it in the end.

> ## Suggested Mini-Lessons
>
> ☐ 1 RHYME SCHEME; NEAR RHYME; INTERNAL RHYME
>
> ☐ 2 METER
>
> ☐ 3 LINKING FORM AND CONTENT
>
> **Materials:** *Copies of pages 80–85 for students.*

Students must read a couple of sample essays (along with the poems the essays explicate) before choosing poems themselves. The first sample essay is about Gwendolyn Brooks's "We Real Cool," a poem that I also use in the mini-lessons to illustrate rhyme and meter. Students can see how our mini-lesson discussions lead to an actual essay. I should also here note that in my experience, "We Real Cool" is the absolute favorite poem of middle school students. There is so much packed into this little poem that it is one of my favorites, too.

Students each choose a poem from a packet of poems that I compiled for both accessibility and potential for deeper meaning. (See Appendix C for poems you could include.) I tried to cover a variety of topics and styles. I have become quite familiar with these poems, and therefore I am better able to help students with them. Most students can find a poem in the packet that interests them. Every year I tweak the packet in an effort to make it even more interesting and accessible.

I have no qualms about explaining entire poems to students if needed. Often a student likes a certain poem but does not understand it at all. During the conference, I ask leading questions and suggest directions in which to think, and I also spell out certain difficult aspects. For example, when once discussing Frost's "Bereft" with a student, I said, "This is a poem about loss. What images give that feeling?" Sometimes, outright explanation can help a student to think deeply about a poem in a way that she otherwise would not have been able to do alone.

Conversely, students are constantly teaching me: one year, a student pointed out that the end of Langston Hughes's "Mother to Son" actually *looked* like a stair, something I had not noticed in my fervor for metaphor, dialect, alliteration, and so on in the poem. During every conference, the student and I trade ideas about the poem he has chosen. This assignment requires me to conference a bit more rigorously than usual, since students need more of my attention.

My goal throughout the year with poetry is to give students the basic tools they need to approach a poem. So often I find that students (and teachers!) are intimidated by poetry. This is not unfounded: poetry takes time to unlock and is often confusing. I tell students that I never fully understand a poem on the first reading, and they shouldn't feel that they have to either. Instead, they can approach a poem with tools they can use to work on it. I want students to feel confident in front of poetry, unafraid that they will "look stupid"—maybe they won't know what a poem's theme is right away, but they can talk about rhyme, meter, alliteration, and simile. They will always have something "smart" to say about a poem. From there, they can relax and really start thinking more deeply about the poem.

Another goal that I have been working on all year, but that I try to drive home during this assignment, is the idea that the form of a poem relates to the content in the poem. For example, the student above who noticed Hughes's last line understood the connection of form and content. I illustrate this concept briefly during the meter mini-lesson, but I work on it more diligently during the individual conferences with each student. Once a student has chosen a poem that interests her, I can ask her specific questions like, "Why do you think there is so much alliteration with the sound "sh" in this poem about the ocean?" or, "This poem is in couplets. Could that relate to the fact that the poem is about two best friends?" Many of the poems in the packet lend themselves to this line of thinking, and the prewriting sheet also leads students to ask these questions.

Although this assignment focuses on rhyme and meter, I include a couple of poems in my packet that are in free verse. I want students to see that free verse is also a form in its own right, one that the poet purposefully chooses. Students who select free verse poems to analyze must explain in their essay why they think the poet chose to use free verse. At all times, I want students to be trying to link form and content. I even entertain a few of the more outlandish student guesses during class discussions in the interest of cultivating this habit.

Like the Short Story Analysis, this assignment requires a sophisticated use of persuasion. Since poetry can be more difficult than fiction, I like to use this essay as the culminating project in the series; it draws on all the skills we have been developing throughout the year.

Mini-Lesson 1
Rhyme Scheme; Near Rhyme; Internal Rhyme

Some students already know what a rhyme scheme is; for most, it's new. They all know what rhyming poems are, and I explain that writers have a way of mapping out the rhyming pattern in a poem. I define rhyme scheme ("a method or code of listing the rhymes in a poem, using letters, starting with *a*") and write a simple illustration on the board:

I quarreled with my brother,
I don't know what about,
One thing led to another
And somehow we fell out.

These lines are the first four lines of Eleanor Farjeon's "The Quarrel," printed in full later in this chapter. We list the rhyme scheme (*abab*), and we look at two poems on a handout—Alfred, Lord Tennyson's "The Eagle" and Theodore Roethke's "My Papa's Waltz" (page 81)—and examine their rhyme schemes. The first stanza of "My Papa's Waltz" contains a near rhyme ("dizzy" and "easy"); I let students discover it themselves and decide what to do. Some students will count it as a rhyme, some won't, and at least one in each class will raise his hand and ask. I take the opportunity to define "near rhyme" on the board: An imperfect rhyme that uses consonance or assonance but does not rhyme completely. I explain that a near rhyme should be counted as a regular rhyme; students add this to their notes and proceed. Another near rhyme can be found in stanza two of the same poem.

When I feel confident that most of the class generally understands how to label a poem's rhyme, I show them Gwendolyn Brooks's "We Real Cool." Students are puzzled: clearly this is a rhyming poem, but all the lines (except the last) end with the word "We." How, then, should they analyze for rhyme, they ask. I tell them to stick with the rules: use only the last word of the line. Thus, the rhyme scheme for this poem is *aaaaaaab*. What about all the rhyme in the middle? It is called "internal rhyme," I explain, and although it doesn't get officially counted in the rhyme scheme, it should be noted in their papers.

At this point, I take a few minutes to explain the assignment. Students will spend the majority of this day flipping through the poetry packet I've put together, looking for a poem to write about. I circulate, helping them understand the poems and choose one they like.

Mini-Lesson 2
Meter

Students recognize that poems have rhythms, and certain poems have stronger rhythms than others. I explain that this, too, can be charted. I teach them an abbreviated form of meter, one that consists only of counting out syllables. I of course realize that meter is much more, and that the stresses in a line are more important than the mere number of syllables; however, in middle school, counting syllables is as good as it gets. I put the same lines from "The Quarrel" on the board as the day before, and we count. I have students list the

numbers as they did with the rhyme scheme letters. These lines have a "meter" of 7, 6, 7, 6, and students can see that a definite pattern exists. I tell them to say the stanza aloud and see if they can feel the meter as well; usually they can. If there is a discrepancy in the meter, (which there often is, since, as I said, meter is based on stressed syllables, not just syllables), I tell students to use their judgment and go with the overall pattern. For example, if a poem that has three stanzas of 8, 6, 8, 6 has a final stanza of 8, 6, 8, 7, students can feel confident saying that the poem generally sticks to the basic meter of 8, 6, 8, 6.

To practice, we look at the poems we used the day before for rhyme scheme: "The Eagle" and "My Papa's Waltz." Students are usually surprised when they realize that "The Eagle" has a perfect eight syllables in every line. "Really, he did this on purpose?" they ask. Some students murmur an appreciative "Wow," while others shake their heads in disbelief, amazed that someone would spend so much time on a poem. Either way, they get a glimpse of the idea that a poem is carefully wrought, literally "made," like a cabinet or a painting. Even the word *line* comes from the Latin word for "linen" and hence "thread"; I like to think of this not only as a visual representation but also an allusion to the craft, the "stitching and unstitching" as William Butler Yeats put it, that goes into poetry. "Think of how much time it takes you to make a chessboard in wood shop," I tell them. When they remember that it takes a whole quarter, they begin to understand. "My Papa's Waltz" is a useful example of a general pattern with a varying syllabic count. (Of course, in reality, each line has three stressed syllables, like a waltz, something I try to explain to any class I think might be able to grasp it.)

Mini-Lesson 3
Linking Form and Content

This is a difficult concept for anyone, but after the first two mini-lessons, students are prepared to make the leap. In addition, if students have been given poems regularly throughout the year and are adept at identifying techniques such as simile, alliteration, personification, and assonance as well as stanzas, they will be even better equipped to attempt this most sophisticated level of poetic comprehension. Linking form and content is not a talent given to a privileged few; it is a skill that can be taught. After learning it, students burst with confidence as if they had been given some secret key to the vault.

All year I stress that poems are not accidents; poets do everything on purpose, or at least *keep* everything in the poem on purpose. (I realize that there are some "accidents" in the writing process, divine inspirations of sorts, but the author still chooses to keep them or cut them in the final drafts.) Readers of poems should ask themselves why the poet chose to do what she did: Why these stanzas? Why free verse? Why this rhyme scheme? Why this meter? Why this alliteration or assonance? Meditate on questions like these, I suggest, and see what comes up.

Understanding this is the heart of a poem; it's what makes poetry different from prose. I want students to realize, as poet Denise Levertov once wrote, that "form is . . . a revelation of content." Seeing the connection between the two demonstrates a solid understanding of the poem on all levels. We look again at Brooks's poem. Students notice that the meter is 4-3-3-3-3-3-3-2. "Mostly 3's," they say. "She was trying for all 3's." "Good," I answer, and continue: "But what if—*what if*—Gwendolyn Brooks changed the meter *on purpose*? What if she made the last line short on purpose? Why, in a poem about these kids and the reckless things they do, would she have a short last line? What does the last line say? Why would it be shorter than the other lines?"

"Oh!" Hands. And more hands. "Because they die soon. So the poem ends soon," one student spouts. "There's no more 'We.' They're dead," another declares. Yes! Now they're understanding the white space. I explain that a poem can create a feeling, not just describe a feeling. A poem can make you experience the feeling as you're reading, not just make you empathize with the speaker. The last line of "We Real Cool" feels short; it feels cut-off, like the young lives of the seven

pool players. If I can get students to understand this, I have taught them one of the great "secrets" and pleasures of poetry.

I've found that almost every poem has some bridge between form and content that middle school students can understand. For example, when teaching Tristam Coffin's "Secret Heart" I ask, "What could be one reason that Coffin chose couplets for this poem?" (Answer: it is about two people, a father and son.) Or when discussing Naomi Long Madgett's "Woman With Flower," I ask, "Why would a poem about letting flowers (and people) grow up on their own instead of smothering them be more effective in free verse?" After reading Felice Holman's "Who Am I," I inquire, "Why are there short, sometimes one-word lines?" (It's a poem about a person being a small but integral piece of the universe.) Then we look at e.e. cummings's "Poem" ("As the cat / climbed over / the top of / / the jamcloset . . .") and I present the same question, expecting, of course, an entirely different answer. After analyzing Robert Frost's "Bereft," I ask, "Why would a poem about not letting go of a lost loved one have a rhyme scheme where the *a* rhyme continues for five lines and then reappears in line eight?" When looking at Lillian Morrison's "The Sidewalk Racer or On the Skateboard" I wonder aloud, "Why does this meter feel fast and rolling?" If a student proposes a connection that I think is a stretch, I go with it: I'd rather that he be trying to see the links than not making any associations at all.

Another (perhaps easier) way to link form and content is through sounds. For example, after we identify alliteration with the letter *s* in Robert Francis's "Like Ghosts of Eagles," I ask, "Why is the *s* sound a good one to alliterate in a poem about rivers?" Or after reading Judith Thurman's "Rags," wherein we've singled out alliteration with the letter *r*, I ask, "Why would alliteration with the letter *r* be effective in a poem about the fierce night wind?"

As always, I help students most during individual conferences. Once a student has chosen a poem, I can take a few minutes to discuss it with her and suggest possible connections.

Assignment 10

Analysis of a Poem

❏ Read the two sample essays and their poems, and write your answers to the questions that go with them.

❏ Browse through the poems I've provided and pick one that you would like to analyze.

❏ Fill out both sides of the prewriting sheet.

❏ On a separate sheet of paper, group your main ideas into paragraphs so you have a map of the essay.

❏ Write a first draft. Your draft should be at least one typed page.

❏ Revise the draft. Check for the following:

_____ an interesting title

_____ an attention-grabbing introduction

_____ quotes from the poem

_____ a strong conclusion

❏ Complete an E/R Check Sheet. Make any changes.

❏ Hand in final copy with the questions, prewriting, groups, drafts, E/R Check Sheet, and this sheet.

		Preliminary Grade	Revised Grade
STRUCTURE (organization, paragraphs, length, font)	20 pts.	_____	_____
PROCESS (questions, prewrite, groups, rough, E/R Check Sheet)	20 pts.	_____	_____
DESCRIPTION (title, intro, conclusion, examples, banned words verbs, transition words, sentence variation)	20 pts.	_____	_____
SPELLING	20 pts.	_____	_____
GRAMMAR (punctuation, capitals, sentences, tense, quotation marks, _____)	20 pts.	_____	_____
	TOTAL		_____

The Quarrel

I quarreled with my brother,
I don't know what about,
One thing led to another
And somehow we fell out.
The start of it was slight,
The end of it was strong,
He said he was right,
I knew he was wrong!

We hated one another.
The afternoon turned black.
Then suddenly my brother
Thumped me on the back,
And said, "Oh, come along!
We can't go on all night—
I was in the wrong."
So he was in the right.

—*Eleanor Farjeon*

The Eagle

He clasps the crag with crooked hands;
Close to the sun in lonely lands,
Ringed with the azure world, he stands.

The wrinkled sea beneath him crawls;
He watches from his mountain walls,
And like a thunderbolt he falls.

—*Alfred, Lord Tennyson*

My Papa's Waltz

The whiskey on your breath
Could make a small boy dizzy;
But I hung on like death:
Such waltzing was not easy.

We romped until the pans
Slid from the kitchen shelf;
My mother's countenance
Could not unfrown itself.

The hand that held my wrist
Was battered on one knuckle;
At every step you missed
My right ear scraped a buckle.

You beat time on my head
With a palm caked hard by dirt.
Then waltzed me off to bed
Still clinging to your shirt.

—*Theodore Roethke*

We Real Cool

The Pool Players.
Seven at the Golden Shovel.

We real cool. We
Skip school. We

Lurk late. We
Strike straight. We

Thin gin. We
Sing sin. We

Jazz June. We
Die soon.

—*Gwendolyn Brooks*

ANALYSIS OF A POEM   SAMPLE ESSAY 1

We Real Cool

The Pool Players.
Seven at the Golden Shovel.

We real cool. We
Left school. We

Lurk late. We
Strike straight. We

Sing sin. We
Thin gin. We

Jazz June. We
Die soon.

—*Gwendolyn Brooks*

Questions:

1. What is the rhyme scheme of this poem?

2. Give an example of:

    alliteration

    internal rhyme

3. What is the meter of the poem?

4. Why does this student think the last line is short?

5. Why does she think the title is ironic?

How to Die Soon

by Noelle Duquette, eighth grader

Dying soon may come fast for many people. Usually you can help that by the way you live your life. When you get into trouble you may die soon. One little mistake can ruin people's lives.

"We Real Cool" is about seven people that dropped out of school and cause trouble. "We / / Lurk late. We / Strike straight" means that they are out at night and causing trouble. "We / Sing sin" shows that they are saying swears. "We / Thin gin" means that they are drinking gin at the Golden Shovel. "We / / Jazz June" explains that they are listening to jazz music, which was rebellious in those days.

The last line says "Die soon." Since that line is shorter than the rest, it is a link that means that the speakers' lives are short, or that they can die any minute for fighting with other people at the Golden Shovel.

The poem has four stanzas. Also, this poem is not free verse; it has a meter and a rhyme scheme. The rhyme scheme is mostly A's but the last line is B. The last line is B because every word at the end of the A lines is "We" and at the last line is "soon." This represents that the kids live as a group, getting into trouble, until they die. There is a lot of alliteration in this poem too, like "Lurk late" and "Jazz June." And there is assonance with the "oo" sound in "cool," "school," and "soon." Finally, words like "late" and "straight" and "sin," "thin" and "gin" are examples of internal rhyming.

The meaning of this poem is that the gangsters drop out of school and get into a lot of trouble which may cause them to die soon. The author may have used the title "We Real Cool" to sound ironic. I think she might have done that because dropping out of school and getting into fights is actually *not* cool.

82

Woman With Flower

I wouldn't coax the plant if I were you.
Such watchful nurturing may do it harm.
Let the soil rest from so much digging
And wait until it's dry before you water it.
The leaf's inclined to find its own direction;
Give it a chance to seek the sunlight for itself.

Much growth is stunted by too careful prodding,
Too eager tenderness.
The things we love we have to learn to leave alone.

—*Naomi Long Madgett*

Questions:

1. Do you think this poem is only about flowers? What could the deeper meaning be?

2. What is the form of this poem?

3. What does this student think the deeper meaning of the flower is?

4. How does the poem's free verse form relate to the theme?

5. How does the student separate lines of poetry in her quote?

Too Much Love

by Ashlee Sweeney, eighth grader

When I first read the poem "Woman With Flower," I pictured a lonely elderly woman tending to the only plant she owned. The woman I imagined was timid and petite. She had thin white hair and obsolete gold glasses. Her eyes were black and her smile huge. She was smiling because she was tending to the flower she raised from a seed. The only problem was that this woman was watching the plant all day, non-stop. The plant couldn't grow because the woman was constantly watching over it. I imagined the speaker was the woman's neighbor telling her to stop overprotecting the plant and to let it flourish on its own, without her help. The speaker says, "The things we love we have to learn to leave alone."

After reviewing the poem, though, I realized that this was only one meaning. This poem could also be about a mother tending a child. The flower could be a child, and the woman a mother. The poem describes the mother being overprotective of her precious child.

I combined the two scenarios I envisioned to find a theme: in order for someone or something to thrive, it needs to be able to explore its surroundings, with no more than a little help. The something or someone needs to be free. That also ties in with the poem's style. The poem was written in free verse, so it has no meter or rhyme. I feel that it was written in free verse because the theme of the poem is freedom.

Remembering the mother-child meaning in the poem, the quote "The leaf's inclined to its own direction; / Give it a chance to seek sunlight by itself" made me realize that it is hard for some parents to let their offspring learn without their helping hands. Being children, we don't realize how hard it must be for them to let us explore new horizons independently.

I would give this poem to any parent. I personally felt this poem was touching. After reading it, I feel like I've understood a little bit of a parent's perspective.

Name _____ Date _____ Period _____

Assignment 10

Analysis of a Poem Prewriting Sheet 1

Title of Poem: _____

Author: _____

Brainstorm: Jot down any thoughts you have about the poem: reactions, ideas, images, or anything else.

_____

_____

_____

_____

_____

_____

_____

_____

Form of Poem:

1. How many stanzas? _____   **2.** Is it free verse? _____ (If Yes, skip questions 3 and 4.)

3. What is the rhyme scheme? _____ **4.** What is the meter? _____

Understanding the poem:

1. Look up any words you don't know and list them and their definitions below.

_____

_____

2. Are there any similes or metaphors? Any personification? List them and their explanations.

_____

_____

3. Is there any alliteration? Any assonance? List it below.

_____

_____

4. Any onomatopoeia? List it below.

_____

_____

5. Is there any word or phrase in the poem that is repeated? List it below.

_____

_____

Assignment 10

Analysis of a Poem Prewriting Sheet 2

6. Are there any sensory details that jump out at you? Could they be symbols for something else?

_____

_____

_____

Line-by-Line Paraphrase: Write some of the lines on the left, and rewrite them in your own words.

Poem	Your own words

Title: What does the title of the poem mean? Could it have a double meaning? What is it?

_____

_____

_____

Theme: What could be a deeper meaning of the poem?

_____

_____

_____

BONUS: Does the form of the poem (line length, alliteration, meter, and so on) relate to the theme or topic? (For example, a poem about silence might have a short last line, to give the feeling of silence. Or a poem about the wind might have alliteration with the letter *s*, to sound like the wind.)

On a separate sheet of loose-leaf paper, group your main ideas into paragraphs.

REMINDERS: Quote parts of the poem as you write. Think of an interesting way to start your analysis.

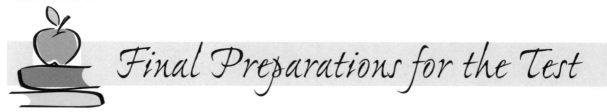

CHAPTER 14

Final Preparations for the Test

SAMPLE ESSAYS

The most effective way to demonstrate how to score well on an essay test is to show students sample essays from each scoring category. These essays may be generated by test makers (or teachers) or, better yet, may be actual student essays from the past that have been published by the state or testing company. Some states post sample essays on their Web sites, or provide study guides that include sample essays. Showing students copies of these essays will greatly enhance their understanding of what is expected of them. In Massachusetts, the middle school essays are given scores ranging from 1–6, 1 being the lowest. Past student essays representing each scoring category are provided on the state's Web site. I print and photocopy a class set of these, and give each student a packet to examine.

Before examining these essays, I give students a copy the corresponding essay question. I also give each student a blank version of the chart on page 87. (For more space, I use a landscape setting.)

We begin with the lowest-scoring essay, and read it as a class. Students then take a few minutes to note the strong and weak points of the essay. We review their answers as a class, and students must add any new ideas from classmates to their own lists. We do the same for the second essay, third, fourth, and so on through the highest-scoring essay. By reading six essays and answering the same question, students can clearly see what skills are rewarded and what mistakes cause deductions. One year, our chart looked like the one on page 87.

The Massachusetts Department of Education (DOE) publicizes its own charts illustrating the scoring process of the essays. However, I find it much more effective to have students compare the essays and deduce for themselves precisely what skills are rewarded at each point level. One element of the higher-scored essays that becomes apparent to students during this exercise is that

length counts. Full paragraphs with examples are a must. The DOE chart won't exactly say, "Length counts!" but will instead use more sophisticated language like, "Idea development" and "Rich topic," which students may or may not understand. Length, of course, does not automatically equal topic richness; my point is that students will learn much more from their own analysis and paraphrasing of the scoring system than they would reading a state-issued list.

If your state does not provide sample essays of each score, it should at least supply schools with the criteria for each score. I would suggest taking this criteria and generating your own essays for students to compare.

PRACTICE QUESTIONS

Another well-known way to prepare students for the test is to have them actually practice some questions. Most states provide sample and/or past essay questions. Having students do dress rehearsals of sorts will tremendously boost confidence and lower anxiety. As much as I can, I make sure students know exactly what to expect, from the question format to the page layout to the actual space provided. I take this information directly from the state's preparation materials.

In Massachusetts, for example, middle school students must write a descriptive essay. On the actual test, there is an introduction that leads to the main question. The introduction is in a box at the top of a page. Students then have four pages of blank paper for a rough draft, followed by four lined pages for a final copy. All of this is provided in the state preparation materials. I instruct students to brainstorm and group on the question page; I tell them to do as much crossing out and rewriting as they wish on the rough draft pages but that they must write neatly on the final draft pages.

I show students as many sample and past questions as I can find. We read them all; I have them brainstorm

	1	2	3	4	5	6
Strengths:	• answered question • used an example	• used paragraphs (but only one sentence each) • used an example	• attempted an intro/concl. • five paragraphs • one idea per paragraph • most words spelled right	• attempted an intro/concl. • paragraphs with one idea and examples • specific examples • sensory details • longest essay so far	• good length • strong introduction • an existing concl. • five paragraphs with one main idea each • many specific examples • no banned words—descriptive words	longest essay • excellent intro • strong concl. • transition words used • six paragraphs with one idea each • many specific examples and sensory details • strong vocab. • sentence variation
Weaknesses:	• too short! only five sentences • no paragraphs • no intro/concl. • fragments—no complete thought • simple words • banned word: "stuff" • simple sentences no variation • more examples	• still much too short • misspellings • no intro/concl. • simple words and sentences • run-ons • example not explained enough • needs more examples	• intro/concl. not effective • many short, choppy sentences • still too short • no sensory details • no specific examples • easy vocabulary and banned words • clichés • the word *is* everywhere	• intro/concl. could be stronger • some clichés • *their* constantly misspelled • some run-ons • banned word: *great*	• concl. could be stronger • *it's* constantly misspelled	• one misspelling • two banned words

and group a few, and fully write out essays for one or two, depending on how many days I can devote to it.

ACRONYMS

Acronyms are some of the oldest mnemonic aids, perhaps because they work so well. I try to invent some before test time to help students remember what they've learned. Two that I use are "By Gosh It's Cold!" and "VEST." One can see how these two complement each other. The first stands for *b*rainstorm, *g*roup, *i*ntroduction, and *c*onclusion: the four main structural elements in essay writing. The second stands for *v*erbs, *e*xamples, *s*entences, and *t*ransition words. The "verbs" category includes verb upgrading and tense continuity. The sentence category refers to sentence variation, as well as run-ons and fragments. Whatever students can remember from any of the letters is a bonus, so I try not to raise anxiety levels by drilling them too hard. I tell myself to trust in the process and the work that's been done all year.

REVISITING AUDIENCE AND TONE

I remind students that they have a very specific audience for the test: adult readers who usually are English teachers during regular school time. Therefore, they should remember to be careful with their tones, and avoid using sarcasm or anger in their voices. Student contempt for having to take the test at all should not seep into their essays. Sometimes, one of the lower-scoring sample essays uses a negative tone; this helps me demonstrate my point. Test graders are looking for skills, I tell students; they have no control over the existence of the test. They are usually teachers doing a bit of extra work in the summer. If students want to protest, I suggest, they can continue writing letters for social change and sending them to the appropriate recipients.

CHECKING MY OWN TONE

Making sure that I stay calm, confident, and positive in the weeks prior to testing time can only benefit students. I try to convert any anxiety or negativity I may have toward the test into something positive. I try not to pass on the pressure that gets put on teachers. I remind myself that good can come from testing, namely, the actual existence of my writing workshop, which would not have happened otherwise. Whatever your situation, take advantage of test pressure as an excuse to carve out more time for writing. We cannot let testing take the little writing time we have and transform it into canned drill sessions. Our responsibility is to help students evolve as writers and thinkers, testing or not.

Spelling Practice Sheet

Write any misspelled words—correctly—five times each.
Hand in this sheet with your revised assignment.

1. _____
2. _____
3. _____
4. _____
5. _____

1. _____
2. _____
3. _____
4. _____
5. _____

1. _____
2. _____
3. _____
4. _____
5. _____

1. _____
2. _____
3. _____
4. _____
5. _____

1. _____
2. _____
3. _____
4. _____
5. _____

1. _____
2. _____
3. _____
4. _____
5. _____

Editing / Revising Check Sheet (1)

Look at your draft, answer these questions, and revise.

	YES	Need to Revise
Do I have an introduction?	❏	❏
Does each paragraph contain **one main idea** with examples?	❏	❏
Do I have a conclusion?	❏	❏
Did I **avoid** banned words such as *good, bad, cool, stuff,* and *thing*?	❏	❏
Did I avoid clichés?	❏	❏
Did I try to use transition words such as *however, although, moreover, consequently,* or *in addition to*?	❏	❏
Did I use the spell-check?	❏	❏
Did I check all commas? (Should they be periods?)	❏	❏
Did I capitalize all names and titles?	❏	❏

Editing / Revising Check Sheet (2)

Look at your draft, answer these questions, and revise.

1. What kind of introduction do I have? (Circle one)

Question   Imagine . . .   Interesting fact   Quote

Sensory detail (sight, sound, smell, taste, touch)   Other (describe) _____

2. What is in my conclusion? (Circle any that apply)

Summary of ideas   Theme or message   Solution to a problem

Opinion   Frame with Introduction

Other (describe) _____

3. Do I have any banned words or clichés? Change them.

What is one banned word I use often? _____

4. Check for at least three transition words. Do I have them? _____

5. Did I check for weak verbs and change some? _____

6. Are my sentences varied? Are they of different lengths with different beginnings? _____
Find one flat sentence and change it.

7. Did I use the spell-check? _____

8. Did I look up any unknown homophones? _____ Name one: _____

9. Check all commas. Should I change any to periods? _____

10. What is one special problem I should check for in my writing? (Write it below and check for it.)

_____

Editing / Revising Check Sheet (3)

Look at your draft, answer these questions, and revise.

1. What technique did I use for my introduction? _____

2. What technique did I use for my conclusion? _____

3. How is my organization? Describe: _____

_____

4. Language: Any banned words? _____ Weak verbs? _____

5. Do I have sentence variation? _____ Transition words? _____

6. What is my tone for this piece? _____

Is it appropriate for the audience? _____

7. Did I use the spell-check? _____

8. Are all my verbs in the same tense? _____

9. What is one punctuation rule I should check for? _____

_____ Check for it.

10. What are two special problems I should check for in my writing?

A _____

B _____

Check for them.

Editing / Revising Check Sheet (4)

Look at your draft, answer these questions and revise.

STRUCTURE/ORGANIZATION

List three areas you should always check, and check them:

	Areas	Checked
1.	_____	❏
2.	_____	❏
3.	_____	❏

DESCRIPTION AND LANGUAGE

List three areas you should always check, and check them.

	Areas	Checked
1.	_____	❏
2.	_____	❏
3.	_____	❏

GRAMMAR AND SPELLING

List three areas you should always check, and check them.

	Areas	Checked
1.	_____	❏
2.	_____	❏
3.	_____	❏

Now list two problem areas that you have been working on this year and check them.

	Areas	Checked
1.	_____	❏
2.	_____	❏

Mini-Lesson Quick Reference

Assignment 1
INTRODUCTORY LETTER
{
1. Brainstorming and Grouping
2. Banned Words
3. E/R Check Sheets

Assignment 2
PROCESS ESSAY
{
1. Sensory Details
2. Ways to End an Essay (Conclusions)
3. Ways to Start an Essay (Introductions)

Assignment 3
COMPARE AND CONTRAST ESSAY
{
1. Compare and Contrast Defined; Possible Organization
2. Clichés
3. Transition Words

Assignment 4
PERSUASIVE ESSAY
{
1. Persuasion Introduced; Potential Topics; Organization
2. Titles
3. Strong Verbs

Assignment 5
LETTER FOR SOCIAL CHANGE
{
1. Explanation of Letter; Topics and Addresses; Envelopes
2. Audience
3. Sentence Variation

Assignment 6
BOOK REVIEW
{
1. Elements of a Book Review
2. How to Have an Opinion About Literature
3. Homophones

Assignment 7
ARTS REVIEW
{
1. Explanation of Review; Topics
2. Tone
3. Commas and Fragments

Assignment 8
PERSONAL ESSAY
{
1. Personal Essay Defined; How to Use a Quotation Dictionary
2. Quoting Within the Essay
3. Words Instead of "Said"

Assignment 9
SHORT STORY ANALYSIS
{
1. Introduction to Analysis; Parts of a Short Story
2. Avoiding "You"
3. Keeping the Same Tense Throughout

Assignment 10
ANALYSIS OF A POEM
{
1. Rhyme Scheme; Near Rhyme; Internal Rhyme
2. Meter
3. Linking Form and Content

Some Persuasive Essay General Topics

You must formulate your own opinion for a main idea.

Laws

Gun control

Use of cell phones while driving

Capital punishment

Working age

Electoral college

Senior drivers

Driving age

Environment

Deforestation, natural resources, pollution

Emissions control

Making smoking illegal

International

Immigration

Child labor in other countries

Global warming

Debt relief for developing nations

Science

Cloning

Product or medical testing on animals

Obesity in the United States

Money spent for NASA explorations

Genetic testing

Schools

Uniforms in public schools

Locker searches

Standardized tests

Homework policies

Mandatory second-language study

Sports

Skateboarding in public places

Eliminating slam dunks

Face masks for all hockey players

American League pitchers hitting in National League games

Video use in refereeing baseball

Expense of Olympics

New sports in Olympics

Professionals in Olympics

Alcohol sales at sporting events

Salary caps in a specific sport

Leisure

Censorship of song lyrics

Violence in video games

Internet monitoring

Words Instead of "Said"

admitted	declared	peeped	snickered
announced	demanded	proposed	snorted
answered	droned	protested	soothed
barked	echoed	purred	spat
bellowed	exclaimed	questioned	sputtered
blabbered	groaned	raged	squawked
blurted	growled	rambled	squeaked
boomed	hissed	recalled	squealed
cackled	hollered	remembered	stammered
chattered	howled	replied	stuttered
chirped	hummed	retorted	swore
chortled	implied	revolted	taunted
chuckled	insulted	roared	threatened
complained	interrupted	sang	translated
complimented	mentioned	scolded	warned
confirmed	moaned	screamed	whined
cooed	mumbled	screeched	whispered
cried	murmured	sighed	yelled
criticized	muttered	slurred	yelped
croaked	offered	snapped	
crooned	panted	sneered	

List of Additional Poem Titles
Arranged by Poetic Technique

Simile or Metaphor

Youth Langston Hughes

Steam Shovel Charles Malam

The Sea James Reeves

Metaphor Eve Merriam

Dreams Langston Hughes

I'm Nobody! Who Are You? Emily Dickinson

Song of the Settlers Jessamyn West

Windy Nights Robert Louis Stevenson

Fire and Ice Robert Frost

Hope is the Thing with Feathers Emily Dickinson

Your World Georgia Douglas Johnson

Alliteration

All But Blind Walter de la Mare

The Sidewalk Racer Lillian Morrison

Preludes T. S. Eliot

Earth Oliver Herford

Like Ghosts of Eagles Robert Francis

The Bird of Night Randall Jarrell

The Base Stealer Robert Francis

Assonance

Widow-Mother Ada Jackson

Stories J. Patrick Lewis

Seashells Douglas Florian

Onomatopoeia

Sonic Boom John Updike

Onomatopoeia Eve Merriam

Fall Wind Aileen Fisher

Personification

The Waking Theodore Roethke

Waiting for the Storm Timothy Steele

Night Francis William Bourdillon

Fog Carl Sandburg

The Breathing Denise Levertov

Sea Lullaby Elinor Wylie

Free Verse

The Hawk Mary Oliver

Gift Czeslaw Milosz

Dog on a Chain Charles Simic

Sisters Lucille Clifton

The Universe May Swenson

Poem William Carlos Williams

Mother to Son Langston Hughes

Pitcher Robert Francis

Lament Edna St. Vincent Millay

Internal Rhyme

Summer Stars Carl Sandburg

The Song by the Way Francisco A. de Icaza

Mean Song Eve Merriam

Snow Toward Evening Melville Cane

Repetition

When I Heard the Learn'd Astronomer Walt Whitman

The Raven Edgar Allan Poe

The Pasture Robert Frost

The Child on the Shore Ursula K. LeGuin

Stopping By Woods on a Snowy Evening Robert Frost

While I Slept Robert Francis

Little Dead Myra Cohn Livingston

End Rhyme & Meter

A Dream Within a Dream Edgar Allan Poe

Nothing Gold Can Stay Robert Frost

A Time to Talk Robert Frost

The Courage That My Mother Had Edna St. Vincent Millay

Richard Cory Edwin Arlington Robinson